Nature is a Battlefield

For Adrienne

Nature is a Battlefield

Towards a Political Ecology

Razmig Keucheyan

Translated by David Broder

polity

First published in French as *La nature est un champ de bataille. Essai d'écologie politique*, (c) Éditions La Découverte, Paris, France, 2014

This English edition (c) Polity Press, 2016

Polity Press
65 Bridge Street
Cambridge CB2 1UR, UK

Polity Press
350 Main Street
Malden, MA 02148, USA

ISBN-13: 978-1-5095-0377-3 (hardback)
ISBN-13: 978-1-5095-0378-0 (paperback)

A catalogue record for this book is available from the British Library.
Typeset in 10.5 on 12 pt Sabon Roman by Toppan Best-set Premedia Limited
Printed and bound in the UK by Clays Ltd, St Ives PLC

Library of Congress Cataloging-in-Publication Data

Names: Keucheyan, Razmig, author.
Title: Nature is a battlefield : towards a political ecology / Razmig Keucheyan.
Other titles: Nature est un champ de bataille. English
Description: Cambridge, UK ; Malden, MA : Polity Press, [2016] | Includes bibliographical references.
Identifiers: LCCN 2016006440 (print) | LCCN 2016018681 (ebook) | ISBN 9781509503773 (hardcover : alk. paper) | ISBN 1509503773 (hardcover : alk. paper) | ISBN 9781509503780 (pbk. : alk. paper) | ISBN 1509503781 (pbk. : alk. paper) | ISBN 9781509503803 (mobi) | ISBN 9781509503810 (epub)
Subjects: LCSH: Political ecology. | Ecology–Political aspects. | Environmental disasters–Political aspects. | Human ecology–Economic aspects. | Environmental justice.
Classification: LCC JA75.8 .K4813 2016 (print) | LCC JA75.8 (ebook) | DDC 304.2–dc23
LC record available at https://lccn.loc.gov/2016006440

The publisher has used its best endeavours to ensure that the URLs for external websites referred to in this book are correct and active at the time of going to press. However, the publisher has no responsibility for the websites and can make no guarantee that a site will remain live or that the content is or will remain appropriate.

Every effort has been made to trace all copyright holders, but if any have been inadvertently overlooked the publisher will be pleased to include any necessary credits in any subsequent reprint or edition.

For further information on Polity, visit our website: politybooks.com

Contents

The experience of our generation: that capitalism will not die a natural death.

Walter Benjamin

Introduction

In Autumn 1982 the inhabitants of Warren County in north-east North Carolina mobilized for six weeks in opposition to a toxic waste landfill being situated in their area.[1] Four years previously, in 1978, an industrial waste management company had illegally dumped large quantities of polychlorinated biphenyl (PCB) – a substance used, among other things, in paint and in electrical transformers. Once these PCBs had been discovered, the state of North Carolina decided to acquire a site where it could bury them and, after looking into many possible locations, it finally opted for one close to the town of Warrenton. As is often the case in this type of situation, local residents opposed the plan, fearing for its impact on their health (as PCBs are carcinogenic substances). They launched a legal bid to stop the waste being dumped in their area but, two years later, the district tribunal rejected their complaint. It was then that the protest took on extra-judicial forms, with demonstrations, sit-ins, boycotts, civil disobedience, marches, meetings, road blockades . . . These actions led to the arrests of over five hundred people, including various local and federal representatives. In the short term, the movement did not succeed in getting the project withdrawn and only in the 2000s would the site be decontaminated.

The arguments that the protestors initially raised in opposition to the landfill site related to the pollution of the

environment (both the water and the soil) by PCBs and the
health risks that this substance posed. Yet as the movement
expanded and became more politicized, the nature of its arguments changed. The residents and their allies insisted that the
state had chosen this site for burying the toxic waste because
it was an area inhabited by Blacks, poor people and above
all poor Blacks. To put it another way, there was a racist basis
for the decision to locate the dump there. At the time, Warren
County had a 64 per cent Black population, with the corresponding figure for the area immediately next to the dump
rising to 75 per cent. In its environmental management and
resources policy, the state systematically favours White populations and the middle and upper classes, which it protects
from this type of harmful substances. Conversely, minorities
– including not only Blacks, but also Native Americans, Hispanics and Asians, as well as the poor – bear the brunt of
industry's negative consequences. We can see that, still today
in the United States, the improper handling of waste in the
vicinity of White neighbourhoods leads to fines five times
more frequently than when it takes place close to Black or
Hispanic ones.[2] This racial discrimination is not necessarily
intentional on the part of the public authorities, even if it
often is so. It is systemic: that is to say, it results from a logic
that is partly independent of individual will. So what allowed
the Warren County movement to reach such scale was its
capacity to generalize, to 'hook' a local demand on to a global
injustice.

This episode is a marvellous illustration of this book's
main argument: namely, that nature is a battlefield. Already
today, it is a battlefield; and in future, as the ecological crisis
deepens, it will increasingly become the theatre of conflicts
among actors with divergent interests: social movements,
states, armies, financial markets, insurers, international organizations . . . In the Warren County case, the conflict resulted
from a particular form of injustice, racism. But it could also
follow from other types of inequalities. Nature is not somehow
free of the power relations in society: rather, it is the most
political of entities.

In approaching the ecological crisis in this manner, we
are clashing with what is today a dominant view; indeed, a
well-established consensus maintains that humanity has to

'overcome its divisions' in order to solve the problem of environmental change. This consensus is driven by ecologist parties, many – if not all – of which emerged in the 1970s, based on the idea that the opposition between Left and Right was obsolete or now of only secondary importance. In France it is also promoted by 'civil society' figures like Yann Arthus-Bertrand and Nicolas Hulot, and there are equivalent personalities in most countries. The 'ecological pact' proposed by Nicolas Hulot – a charter signed by several of the candidates for the 2007 French presidential election, as well as many thousands of citizens – is typical of this conception of ecology.[3] This consensus is also the backdrop to the dissatisfaction over the recurrent failure of international climate talks – most recently in Copenhagen and Rio. Such complaints are a moral condemnation of states' incapacity to come together over common environmental objectives.

There are more sophisticated versions of this ecological consensus. One of the leading theorists of postcolonialism and author of the classic *Provincializing Europe*, Dipesh Chakrabarty,[4] has recently published a text entitled 'The Climate of History'.[5] In his eyes, the ecological crisis allows us to see for the first time the prospect of humanity as such and not one of its component parts – workers, peasants, the colonized, women . . . – becoming the 'subject' of history. We humans never experience ourselves as a 'species', since all experience is always singular, even if it is collective. Yet in Chakrabarty's view, climate change means the emergence of conditions in which humanity must act in common in order to respond to the challenge of global warming; and this should thus lead us to re-evaluate the old notion of humanism, to which this challenge grants unprecedented significance. It should also lead us to re-evaluate the critiques of this notion, in particular the ones that (post)structuralism levelled against it from the 1960s onward. The 'theoretical anti-humanism' of Louis Althusser or of Michel Foucault's *The Order of Things* takes on different meaning when the survival of humanity is under threat from climate upheavals.

Comparing the economic and ecological crises, Chakrabarty states that 'Unlike in the crises of capitalism, there are no lifeboats here [within the context of climate change] for the rich and the privileged.'[6] The rich will always do well out of economic crisis but, according to Chakrabarty, this will not be the case with the ecological crisis, since there will be no 'lifeboat' allowing them to leave the planet. Even though Chakrabarty does recognize that this crisis also entails a class dimension, in the sense that its impact is not evenly distributed across the population, he maintains that in the last instance it transcends this dimension and that the question of humanity must therefore be put back on the agenda. As such, he argues that 'the current crisis has brought into view certain other conditions for the existence of life in the human form that have no intrinsic connection to the logics of capitalist, nationalist, or socialist identities'.[7] To say the least, this idea is rather surprising coming as it does from postcolonial studies, which have made a specialty out of rejecting all forms of universalism.[8]

Our analysis starts from a hypothesis that is exactly the inverse of Chakrabarty's. If we take seriously the idea that since the mid eighteenth century climate change has been brought on by economic development, and that this development is called 'capitalism', then it is unlikely that we will be able to transcend our class oppositions before we find a solution to the environmental crisis. In other words, it is unlikely that rallying the human species around common objectives is a condition of resolving this crisis. Rather, its solution may well require the radicalization of these oppositions – that is, the radicalization of the critique of capitalism. The one divides into two, in environmental matters as with so many others.

Our first chapter is entitled 'Environmental Racism'. It will allow us to demolish the idea that humanity suffers the consequences of the ecological crisis in a uniform way. Just as there are economic and cultural inequalities, we also find inequalities in individuals' or groups of individuals' relation to nature and to the resources that it offers, and in their exposure to the harmful effects of development: pollution, natural and industrial disasters, water quality, access to energy . . . In certain cases, environmental inequalities are the result of the actions of states, whose policies are far from neutral in this regard, as we saw in the Warren County example. In other cases, they are the fruit of market logic being left to its own devices. In still other cases, they are the outcome of inextricably linked economic and political logics.

The 'intersectionality' of gender, race and class, which is today the object of numerous works,[9] must therefore be completed by a fourth, complicating dimension: nature. This latter itself possesses a highly problematic (political) ontology, which can only be conceived in dialectical relation with these three other dimensions. Here we will concentrate on the question of environmental racism – that is, on the intersection between 'nature' and 'race'. Even so, we can only properly understand this phenomenon on condition that we take into account the whole set of inequalities that are at work within the system.

Throughout capitalism's existence, faced with crisis situations and the aggravated inequalities that they engender, it has resorted to the two solutions of financialization and war. In generating 'fictitious' capital, finance allows for the deferral and thus the temporary attenuation of the contradictions inherent to capitalist production (as its subprime lending mechanism recently once again demonstrated). War is the fruit of the inevitable conflicts that these contradictions periodically generate. The shrinking of profit opportunities and the need to guarantee control over the extraction and circulation of resources – but also the growing opposition to the system – tend to make political conflictuality increasingly acute. In (literally) destroying capital, war also makes it possible to restart accumulation on new bases.[10]

The ecological crisis is a further case in which capitalism is putting these two solutions into effect. In other words – as this book will seek to demonstrate – financialization and militarization are the system's two reactions to this crisis. The second chapter ('Financializing Nature: Insuring Climatic Risks') concerns the insurance covering the climatic threat, which is today one of the main forms that environmental finance takes. We are currently seeing a proliferation of 'trendy' financial products related to nature or biodiversity: carbon markets, climate derivatives, catastrophe bonds . . . These products are aimed at mortgaging or managing the social and economic turbulence that results from the ecological crisis. They nevertheless also have the objective of making a profit from it. They are part of the financialization of capitalism that is now underway: and as we shall see, this also involves the financialization of nature. For capitalism, nature is today the object of an *accumulation strategy*.

Capitalism is an ambivalent system and insurance is a centrally important component of this mechanism. On the one hand, capitalism is unstable, since it generates innovation (the 'creative destruction' so dear to Joseph Schumpeter), globalization, class struggle and processes that exercise a corrosive effect on social order. As Marx and Engels put it in the *Communist Manifesto*:

> Constant revolutionising of production, uninterrupted disturbance of all social conditions, everlasting uncertainty and agitation distinguish the bourgeois epoch from all earlier ones . . . All that is solid melts into air.[11]

On the other hand, capitalism requires stability, since investment and the construction of profitable markets would be inconceivable without this. How is it possible to reconcile the system's two contradictory characteristics, instability and stability? Well, in good measure it is thanks to the mechanism of insurance. This mechanism is what makes it possible to take financial risks, while also protecting the investment when things turn bad. But what happens to this insurance mechanism in a context being made increasingly uncertain by environmental crisis?

The third chapter ('Green Wars, or the Militarization of Ecology') looks at the growing interconnection between war and ecology. The capitalist exploitation of nature influences the manner in which armed conflicts develop. The environmental crisis resulting from this exploitation has already led to a rise in natural disasters, the increasing scarcity of certain resources, food crises, a destabilization of the poles and oceans, as well as the multiplication of 'climate refugees', set to number in the tens of millions by 2050. The result is *green wars* or *climate wars* – the translation of the ecological crisis onto the terrain of war. States in general and armies in particular are in the front line of the very particular 'negative externality' of armed conflicts. The ecological crisis is not only being financialized, but also entails the potentiality of armed conflicts.

Military figures are conscious of this growing interconnection between war and ecology. Across the last decade or so the planet's major armed forces, with the US Army first among them, have been producing reports devoted to the impact that climate change will bear on military strategy. What consequences will this change have for the way in which war is fought? If we accept that the environment is a crucial factor in any war situation, then the upheavals that it is going to go through – and is already undergoing – on account of the ecological crisis will necessarily influence the art of war. In short, Sun Tzu and Clausewitz are being ecologized.[12]

1

Environmental Racism

Reforestation is the means by which our race will conserve
its European faculties.
    François Trottier, *Reboisement et colonisation* (1876)

The Warren County episode to which I referred in the Introduction was the founding act of the environmental justice
movement and the starting point for a whole cycle of protests.
And while one of the first expressions of this movement arose
in the USA, it also has major international ramifications. After
all, this movement's most important characteristic is the fact
that it sets the social – gender, race and class – in relation with
nature. It is also in dialogue with other contemporary ecologist currents, for example the movement for climate justice.[1]
This latter has established the correspondence between climate
crisis, the inequalities between North and South and the logic
of centre and periphery. Among its most important demands
is the recognition of the 'ecological debt' the countries of the
North owe those in the South, having racked up this liability
across the colonial and postcolonial periods.[2]
    For its part, the environmental justice movement's strug-
gles have to do with climate change and its consequences, but
also the environment more generally: including toxic waste,
pollution, access to amenities, workplace safety and so on.
Characteristic of this movement is the fact that it poses the

question of ecological inequalities not at the global level, like the climate justice movement, but at a national level. These inequalities are inherent in the construction of modern nation-states but have long been rendered invisible on account of the greater prominence of other types of inequality; the neglect of environmental questions by large parts of society and, in particular, by the workers' movement; and the idea that nature is a universal good accessible to all regardless of gender, race or class. Yet on closer inspection we see that nothing could be further from the truth.

The environmental justice movement did not come out of the ecology movement that emerged in the 1950s or the environmentalist movement that first appeared in the nineteenth century; rather, it emerged from the civil rights movement. It was a belated consequence of this struggle, an unexpected offshoot that appeared in the last third of the twentieth century at a time when the civil rights movement was losing momentum. Like the civil rights struggle, it first arose and developed in the US South, before then spreading throughout the country. Moreover, the means that it used – its 'repertoire of action' – were largely inspired by this earlier struggle for civil rights, with its trademark sit-ins, boycotts, marches, road blockades, etc. Characteristic of this repertoire of action is its foundational commitment to pacifism, seeking to demonstrate that it is the system – and not the movement challenging it – that resorts to violence and repression. Traditional environmentalism in the United States has been notably characterized by its legalism, that is, by its often 'technical' or 'expert' approach to environmental problems (also in this sense differing from the means used by its European counterparts). The first generation of the environmental justice movement's leaders largely came from the civil rights struggle. Indeed, the question of waste management had already arisen within this movement. On the eve of his assassination in April 1968, Martin Luther King visited Memphis to support the strike action being pursued by mainly Black sanitation workers, who had walked out in protest at their dangerous and unhygienic working conditions as well as against low wages.

Poorer sections of the population and racial minorities are in general less likely to take legal action to stop toxic waste being dumped close to their neighbourhoods. Indeed, this is one of the reasons why the state so often offloads this waste in these areas. Because these people are less well endowed with various kinds of 'capital' – in a Bourdieusian sense – they are less able to mobilize effectively and build movements. In contrast, the representatives of higher classes know how to deploy the law to make themselves heard and how to play on politicians' fears of being punished at the ballot box. Nor is the NIMBYism so decried by the mainstream ecology movement – strategies for avoiding private sacrifices that are to the detriment of the (real or supposed) general interest – evenly distributed across the whole population. Rather, it reflects factors of gender, race and class. The Warren County protest did also include Whites, such as the farmers opposed to the PCBs polluting their land; and, like any sizeable social protest movement, it was a heterogeneous coalition of interests and demands. But what was most notable about this movement was the fact that it exposed the racial and social injustice underlying the management of toxic waste.

A philosophical event

Antonio Gramsci wrote in his *Prison Notebooks* that the Russian Revolution was a 'philosophical event' – it had consequences not only on the political terrain, but also at the level of thought itself.[3] The environmental justice movement was also the starting point of a cycle of fruitful theoretical elaborations. *Toxic Waste and Race in the United States* was one study that made a particular splash, appearing in the wake of the Warren County episode and similar mobilizations. It was the first study to establish analytically what the North Carolina protestors had already seen on the ground: that in the USA race is one of the factors that explains why toxic waste is dumped where it is – and in many cases, the main factor. If you want to know where a stock of toxic waste is most likely to be discharged, then ask yourself where Blacks, Hispanics, Native Americans and other racial minorities live. And also ask yourself where the poor neighbourhoods are. This study was produced by the United Church of Christ, a progressive Black congregation that was very active in the civil rights movement in the 1950s. Indeed, as in the case of the civil rights struggle, churches play a crucial role in the environmental justice movement. From the era of slavery onward, Blacks have been deprived of any autonomous political institutions of their own and churches have therefore played an organizing role in their liberation movements. They have been vectors of struggle.[4] Indeed, some of them have been in the vanguard of addressing ecological problems.

The United Church of Christ's study clearly demonstrated the existence of 'environmental racism' in the United States. This expression – indeed, one destined to a great future – is today the object of academic as well as political discussions. The theoretical interest in environmental racism is one consequence of the environmental justice movement. It is a 'philosophical event' in Gramsci's sense of the term.

It was the Reverend Benjamin Chavis – coordinator of the United Church of Christ's report – who first coined the notion of 'environmental racism', establishing the connection between race and toxic waste. At that time Chavis was the leader of that church's 'racial justice' commission; indeed, he was a leading figure in the civil rights movement and an aide to Martin Luther King. During the 1990s he became executive director of the National Association for the Advancement of Colored People (NAACP), the body co-founded by W. E. B. Du Bois at the beginning of the twentieth century. Previous to that, Chavis had also been one of the 'Wilmington Ten', a group of civil rights activists imprisoned at the beginning of the 1970s; there was an international campaign for their release, whose prominent supporters included Amnesty International. As such, Chavis in many ways embodied the link between the civil rights movement and environmental justice.

This movement had an impact on the legislative agenda of subsequent decades and, in February 1994, President Bill Clinton signed Executive Order 12898, which made environmental justice a stated objective of federal policies. This decree bound the state to fighting environmental inequalities wherever they blighted the lives of racial minorities and the most deprived. In 1995 the federal government's Environmental Protection Agency (EPA) published an *Environmental Justice Strategy* declaring that no social or ethnic group should have to put up with a 'disproportionate' share of ecological damage; or, to put it another way, its detrimental effects should be spread out as equitably as possible. It also stated that the elaboration of environmental policies at the different levels of government should involve all parts of society as stakeholders.[5] However, this *Strategy*'s stipulations largely remained a dead letter. Legislation in this field tended to naturalize environmental inequalities; that is, to represent them as an inevitable consequence of economic development, whose baleful impact merely ought to be spread out less unfairly. The movement for environmental justice, however, took a less complacent, more radical approach to these inequalities.

The colour of ecology

Of course, it is the racial dimension of the civil rights move-ment that explains why the movement for environmental justice originally emanated from this struggle. However, a further factor was the traditional US environmentalist organizations' almost total lack of concern for racial questions.

In the mid 1980s the Los Angeles mayor's office decided to site an incinerator in the city's poor, Black and Hispanic-majority South Central neighbourhood. The author-ities claimed that this project would encourage development in this area and generate employment. However, a report on the incinerator's environmental impact predicted that it would give off toxic substances (in particular dioxins, which are also carcinogenic) and that this would have potentially serious consequences for the health of those living nearby.[6] As in the case of Warren County, the neighbourhood's residents mobi-lized to block the project. Seeking to get a coalition off the ground, they made contact with representatives of the coun-try's most important environmental organizations. In the USA these are collectively known as the Group of Ten, a group that includes the Sierra Club, the Audubon Society, the Wilderness Society, the WWF and the Environmental Defence Fund, each of which is something between a lobby group and a mass organization. Some of them were established a long time ago – for example, the Sierra Club was founded in 1892 by John Muir (1838–1914), often described as the father of US environmentalism – and they picked up strength again in the 1960s and 1970s, as they were swept along by the growth of the ecology movement. The Sierra Club today counts more than 1.5 million members. According to its mission statement, its objective is to 'Explore, enjoy and protect the wild places of the earth.'[7]

These associations refused to join the coalition that the South Central residents were trying to build, responding that the installation of an incinerator in an urban setting was a 'community health issue', not an 'environmental' problem.[8] That is not to say that they supported its construction; they thought that it simply wasn't their business to oppose it. This episode was not the first time that class and race relations knocked on the door of mainstream US environmentalism, only for it to remain shut. Already in 1972, under pressure from the civil rights movement and other social struggles of the day, the Sierra Club conducted a survey among its members, seeking to find out whether they wanted their association to develop policies specifically regarding minorities and the poor. Two-thirds of them replied in the negative.[9] The recurrent argument underlying this view asserts that nature is a universal good that anyone can enjoy, regardless of any other differences. Setting specific policies would thus conflict with the 'transcendent' character of Man's relation to nature.

On this occasion, the Sierra Club's survey also undertook a census of its membership. This showed that the vast majority of them were White and drawn from the middle and upper classes. At that time, the boards of the Group of Ten associations did not include a single representative of the US's racial minorities. This was what the Black sociologist Robert Bullard – one of the organic intellectuals of the environmental justice movement and author of the classic *Dumping in Dixie. Race, Class and Environmental Quality* – called the 'environmental élitism' of the dominant ecology movements.[10] The colour of ecology is not green, but White.

The South Central episode was in many ways symptomatic. The 'environment' seemed to lie beyond the relations among social forces. Yet nothing could be more political.

Indeed, a number of genealogical inquiries in recent years have investigated the concept of 'the environment' – as a scientific, philosophical, administrative, or some other type of category.[11] This notion also has a different meaning in each country: indeed, insofar as the environment is constructed in and through public policies, its contours have been shaped by the nation-state as a political form. It is also a class concept, which in problematizing a certain range of problems, also excludes others. So for mainstream US environmentalism, the community health issues raised by the siting of an incinerator in a working-class neighbourhood are not environmental matters. As the Sierra Club mission statement mentioned above has it, an environmental question worthy of the name is one that affects a supposedly virgin 'wilderness' that man has destroyed or despoiled, which the association proposes to return to its original purity. So this immediately defines the category 'environmental issues' in a way that excludes urban questions; and this separation between towns and nature has played a decisive role in the environmentalist movement in most Western countries.

In the United States as elsewhere, the popular classes and ethnic minorities are concentrated in urban areas, whether in inner-cities or on the city periphery. In walling the social off from the natural, the Group of Ten also erect a barrier between the urban and the rural. In contrast, precisely what the environmental justice movement is trying to do is to tear down this barrier: after all, this movement is firmly rooted in the urban context. This current is often described in terms of 'ecopopulism' – a populism in the original sense of an anti-élitist popular movement that uses a representation of the past to critique the present.[12] Yet the historical forms of populism in the USA and Russia had a very marked agrarian component. As such, we can only really apply the term 'ecopopulism' to the environmental justice movement on condition that we also emphasize its urban dimension. A common witticism in this movement holds that Blacks are themselves an 'endangered species', no less than dolphins or the bald eagle, the emblematic bird of the USA. This joke subverts a central utterance of the ecology movement in order to attract attention to the link between racial and environmental questions.

Hurricane Katrina as a 'metaphor' for environmental racism

Hurricane Katrina, which struck New Orleans in August 2005, was particularly revealing in this regard, serving as a 'metaphor' for environmental racism. The whole series of racial and environmental parameters described above were now concentrated in a specific time and place.

Hurricane Katrina flooded close to 80 per cent of New Orleans' land area, with the water level sometimes reaching as high as 7.5 metres. A good part of the city is situated below sea level, with property development also having spread out into the coastal wetlands – a buffer zone between the city and the ocean. The human cost of Katrina was some 2,000 confirmed fatalities. It is highly likely that the real death toll was much higher. More than a million people took refuge in the states neighbouring Louisiana, some of them for good: a third of them would never return to New Orleans.[13] Looting in the days and weeks that followed led to a National Guard intervention, with some 65,000 soldiers coming to take control of shops and other premises.[14] Katrina also provided the city and state authorities with an opportunity to accelerate the gentrification of New Orleans, further expelling poor and minority populations from inner-city neighbourhoods: a classic example of what Naomi Klein calls 'shock therapy'.[15]

Who were Katrina's victims? This question is the key to understanding the relation between social inequalities and natural disasters, in the USA but also more generally. It would be some scientific achievement to produce a comprehensive statistical response to this question, since the available data is either full of gaps or difficult to obtain from the relevant authorities. The first series of the TV series *Treme* is telling in this regard. It portrays a female character – named LaDonna Batiste-Williams – trying to find out what happened to her brother in the hurricane: was he dead, was he in prison, or had he moved to another city? *Treme* was the work of the same producer as *The Wire* and shared the same realism. The struggle that this character faces trying to find a loved one reflects many families' experience following this catastrophe.

The available data show that two categories were over-represented among the victims: Blacks and, most of all, the elderly.[16] Old people are the first victims of this kind of event, at least in industrialized countries; another example would be the 2003 heatwave that swept across continental Europe. By definition, elderly people are less mobile, because of their more fragile health and greater isolation. Add to this the fact that given their fragility, old people's first reaction to a catastrophe will likely be to stay at home, and this often proves fatal.

But what explains the over-representation of Blacks among the victims – not only among the dead, but also among the people who disappeared? According to the available statistics 68 per cent of the pre-Katrina New Orleans population were Black and they represented some 84 per cent of those who went missing after Katrina.[17] The hardest-hit neighbourhoods were also the most racially segregated: indeed, Black neighbourhoods are often located in the areas most prone to immediate flooding. Conversely, the ruling classes tend to make their homes at higher altitude. And Katrina was not the first time that New Orleans had been hit by flooding. Indeed, there is a collective memory of such disasters and this is spatially expressed in the city's particular division of territory among the social classes, exposing some of them to greater danger while protecting others. Blacks were also less likely to receive emergency assistance and, even when they did get it, this help arrived less quickly. Conversely, they were much more likely to be targeted by the National Guard's efforts at 'pacifying' the city. The racial factor is also closely tied to the element of class. The poor are less likely to own their own cars, making it more difficult for them to flee from such disasters.

An event like Katrina has immediate effects, but also more long-term consequences for those who remain in the area afterward. The hurricane generated some 80 million cubic metres of debris of various kinds, from the most organic to the most artificial – some ten times more than the 9/11 attacks did.[18] Add to this picture the 350,000 cars and 60,000 boats swept away by the floods, whose fuel and electronic fittings were dumped into the water; and also the more than 50,000 tonnes of toxic waste from the factories

surrounding the city. All this led to a long-term contamina-
tion of the soil, with definite health consequences for New
Orleans residents. The name for vegetables from the city
allotments tended by working-class residents is 'Katrina
Salad', which puts an ironic spin on the toxic substances
that they contain.[19]

The spatiality of racism

The notion of environmental racism allows us to appreciate
the inequalities in the ways in which different social groups
relate to the environment. More than that, it also allows us
to progress in our understanding of what racism is. Racism
is not a simple question of racist opinions or racist intentions,
even if it is also that. In the modern era it has a systemic
dimension. That means that independently of their own
thinking, certain categories of individual benefit from the
logic of racism – that is, from the fact that they are on the
'right' side of the discriminations that others suffer. This
systemic dimension of racism has many different variants: in
the case that interests us here, it is expressed by the fact that
racism has a *spatiality* – the fact that it is deployed spatially.
As the most sophisticated theorist of environmental racism,
Laura Pulido, has put it, there is a 'spatial sedimentation of
racial inequalities'.[20] Be it rural or urban, space is structured
according to racial fracture lines. The geological metaphor
of 'sedimentation' implies that this is a process embedded in
the *longue durée*, leading to the hardening of differentiated
social-spatial 'layers'. The space in question is simultaneously
both social and natural; for as we have seen, the logic of
capital snatches hold of natural resources.

Racism is a 'multi-scalar' phenomenon playing out across
many different scales: that of the individual and her ideology;
that of the market and its logic of allocating goods; that of
the state and the public policies that it implements, for
example in terms of handling toxic waste; and finally the level
of international relations and imperialism. These scales constantly interact and bump in to one another. The more we
pass from the microsocial to the macrosocial level, the more
the forces at work are abstract ones and the further removed

they are from individuals' intentionality – not that that means that they stop being racist.[21]

Let's imagine a polluting company setting up near a Black neighbourhood in the United States, or next to a suburban housing scheme in a major French city, where most of the inhabitants are of immigrant descent. And let's say, hypothetically, that the business's decision to move to this particular location is motivated by the sole criterion of real estate prices – on which count, this site is far superior to any alternative one. So this is a 'rational' choice in the sense that neoclassical economics would have it (in so-called 'rational choice' theory). Is this, then, a racist decision? Not if we stick to the criterion of intention, since this company's only intention is to minimize its outgoings.

The problem with that, however, is that the price of real estate is itself closely correlated to the 'spatial sedimentation of racial inequalities' that Laura Pulido discusses. This location is far preferable to the rest in price terms because of its proximity to segregated populations and the negative social significations attached to these populations and the neighbourhoods where they live. These significations may themselves give rise to more or less inadequate infrastructure and public services. In this sense, the market is a far from neutral allocation mechanism. The process by which property prices are constituted internalizes not only pollution, but also the logic of racism. That is why if we want to understand racism, then it is not enough to busy ourselves with opinions and intentions. Rather, we need a systemic point of view, for this alone can grasp this phenomenon's multi-scalar dimension.

Naturally, the racial variable is not an isolated one and it is mixed in with other variables – especially that of class. We can see this when we compare the environmental racism to which Blacks and Latinos fall victim in Los Angeles.[22] These two categories of the population are over-exposed to industrial hazards, in particular pollution and toxic waste and to degraded environmental conditions. But not for the same reasons in both cases. Latinos in Los Angeles have historically constituted a cheap workforce. The history of waves of migration from Latin America is inextricably linked to the region's industrial history. Latinos have always lived near industrial areas and have been employed *en masse* in industry (whether legally or illegally). The fact that they have been, and remain, victims of industrial hazards is principally due to their place in the production process and the racial division of labour that sets them at the very bottom of the wages hierarchy.

Historically, Blacks have not played this same role as a cheap workforce for the city's industry. Or, more accurately, they have done so, but intermittently. In fact, they have often lived in deindustrialized neighbourhoods, some of which are ghettoes without any industrial life. When they are victims of environmental racism it is because these neighbourhoods attract polluting installations, typically meaning waste incinerators. So unlike for Latinos, this owes more to the fact that they live in massively segregated neighbourhoods, than due to their place in the racial division of labour. As such, the class factor – in the sense of their position in social stratification – plays a more important role in the Latinos' case.

Conversely, even if race and class are both important to each of the two cases, the race factor is the decisive one when it comes to the Black population. Race is liable to produce differentiation within a class position and, in turn, class is liable to produce differentiation within a given ethno-racial belonging.[23] In this regard, it is interesting to note the fact that White workers long ago abandoned the neighbourhoods in question – the Latino *barrio* and the Black ghetto – in order to move into locations less exposed to industrial hazards. This shows that in the Los Angeles case environmental inequalities cannot be explained in terms of class alone.

We can see also a spatial–racial segmentation of the labour market in France.[24] Ethno-racial belonging and the modalities of occupying space (spatial segregation) interact in a way that impacts on unemployment rates, wage gaps, work careers and even the very different working conditions for those belonging to the 'majority population', as compared to Maghrebian, African or Turkish migrants or the descendants of immigrants. Moreover, these spatial–racial inequalities have barely diminished over time. Hence we can see that since 1975 in France there has been an increase in the unemployment rate gap between 'natives' and immigrants and that the intersection of racial, spatial and class variables in many ways explains this.

Lead poisoning and class struggle

Environmental racism is not a uniquely US phenomenon: far from it. Its logic plays out in all four corners of the planet, in various different forms. For example, we can see one expression of this logic in Great Britain, in a translation of its national history: a *rural racism*.[25] Historically, the countryside was decisively important to the construction of the English ruling classes' identity and in their experience of Englishness. The gentry took form in a certain relation to nature: and this in part explains the fact that it is so strongly identified with land ownership, on the economic as well as the cultural plane. The popular classes – but also the peoples of the Empire who became ethno-racial minorities in Britain – were excluded from this privileged relationship; and this situation has continued to this day.[26] That is the reason why since the 1980s organizations in Britain close to the environmental justice movement, such as the Black Environmental Network, have organized trips taking these minorities to visit the countryside.[27] This provides them with an opportunity to familiarize themselves with a context to which they are usually foreigners and thus to break through the upper classes' monopoly connection with nature. This also provides them an opportunity to get stuck in to activities like 'cultural gardening', where they can grow plants from their own country of origin and thus use nature as a means of keeping alive their ties with that country.

Inequalities of this kind are also at work in France, even if studies on this phenomenon are much less numerous and thus less widely known than in the Anglo-Saxon world. For example, ecological inequalities are found throughout the Île-de-France [Paris and the surrounding region]. Such inequalities are found in a range of environmental variables, breaking down into environmental 'resources' – bodies of water and waterways, green spaces and protected spaces, forests – and environmental 'liabilities' – nitrogen dioxide (NO_2) levels, pollution, flood zones, factories classed under the Seveso Directive, airport, railway and road noise . . .[28] We can also see such inequalities in five sociological variables concerning the *communes* of Île-de-France: the proportion of

people in managerial and intermediate and higher profes-
sional occupations; the *commune*'s average income per inhabitant; the unemployment rate; and the proportion of renters
and social housing tenants. This second series of variables
allows us to determine the relative wealth of a territory and
its inhabitants.

What happens when these two sets of variables are juxta-
posed – when the map of environmental resources and handi-
caps is placed on top of the map of the social terrain? The
traditionally noted geographical separation between Paris's
wealthier Western suburbs and the less fortunate ones to the
East clearly also entails an environmental dimension. The
communes with the most unfavourable ecological situation
are mainly situated in Northern and Eastern Paris, in Seine-
Saint-Denis, the northern part of Hauts-de-Seine, the southeast of the Val-d'Oise and in the area around Roissy airport.
The ones with the most favourable situation are to the South
and West of the region. Thus '45.5 per cent of *communes*
belonging to the category "good environmental quality" are
communes that present the very uppermost socio-urban
profile in Île-de-France . . . [whereas] close to 50 per cent of
communes in the worst environmental quality category
belong to the lowest socio-urban classification'.[29] Statistically,
communes whose territory encompasses *Zones urbaines sensibles* (ZUS)[30] tend to have even poorer environmental quality.

However, on closer inspection we see that the situation is
rather more complex. Sometimes an amenity like a local
natural park or a lake may stand not far from a working-class
district and, conversely, some relatively rich *communes* may
be subject to the presence of a flood zone or the noise from
an airport. As such, we need a subtler analysis of the environmental variables in question. Such an analysis will allow
us to grasp a decisively important aspect of the logic of environmental inequalities in this region. Four main variables
underpin the environmental inequalities among the different
parts of Île-de-France: protected spaces, industrial hazards
classed under the Seveso Directive, noise from railways and
noise from airports. It is these factors that explain the divides
among neighbourhoods with more and less advantageous
positions on the environmental plane. The other variables do
also count, but to a lesser extent.

Three of these four variables concern the category 'liabilities', with the exception being protected spaces (namely, historic sites and monuments and architectural and landscape heritage). A neighbourhood situated on the 'good' side of environmental inequalities will therefore be characterized not so much by its possession of particular ecological resources as by the absence of environmental liabilities. As such, environmental inequalities are the result of a 'negative' process.

Environmental inequalities in the Île-de-France region also entail a racial dimension.[31] To take one example, this is apparent in the case of lead poisoning, an old disease that made its reappearance in Paris in the 1980s.[32] Lead poisoning did not re-emerge just anywhere. It mainly appeared in old and decaying habitats like the ones we find in the city's working-class neighbourhoods, and it was the population categories living in such apartment blocks who were affected; in that period, specifically meaning immigrants from sub-Saharan Africa. A study carried out for the Paris mayor's office in 2002 surveyed more than a thousand unsanitary buildings in the capital.[33] Eighty per cent of the people living there were immigrants, a third of whom were undocumented. This was a very poor population, with 40 per cent of them living on an income of less than €300 a month.

The 1980s saw the reappearance of lead poisoning above all among children. It creates neurological problems in small children, as well as developmental abnormalities. The cause of this poisoning is the intoxication of children by lead, which was used in the paint in apartment blocks until its use was banned in the mid twentieth century. The lead is still present in those buildings that have not been renovated since that time; and poisoning results from the ingestion of flakes and dust from the paint. So we can see that the air we breathe has an eminently political content. The lower we stand on the scale of inequalities, the worse the air quality. The unsanitary conditions in these blocks also stir up other pathologies: allergies, respiratory or skin complaints and so on. So there is evidently a social and racial geography of epidemics, conforming to the contours of working-class neighbourhoods and the most precarious populations.

Recognition of this geography only came belatedly. The fact that it mainly affected sub-Saharan populations initially gave rise to the 'culturalist' explanations provided by the media and the public powers. So, for example, we heard that there was lead in African objects used to decorate these dwellings, or even that the structure of the African families concerned – large families, polygamy, etc. – meant children being left to their own devices. Comparative epidemiology shattered such claims. If in France it is sub-Saharan Africans who are affected by this disease, in Britain it is children of Indian or Pakistani origin and, in the United States, Black children.[34] The conclusion? It's nothing to do with culture and everything to do with an immigrant minority's status, spatial segregation and its class position.

As it happens, immigrants are not the only victims of lead poisoning: it also depends on the region concerned. Situated in Nord-Pas-de-Calais, the Metaleurop Nord factory – which was placed in liquidation in 2003 – had been producing lead and zinc ever since 1894.[35] From then onward it released large volumes of toxic substances into the atmosphere: lead, cadmium, zinc, sulphur hydroxide . . . A series of studies conducted in Nord-Pas-de-Calais have demonstrated that 10 per cent of children in this region have abnormally high amounts of lead in their blood; meanwhile, thirty-six Metaleurop employees were victims of lead poisoning in the late 1990s. Property market prices now also reflect these pollution levels, following the same logic that we described above. Indeed, we can see that in this region a property loses 20 per cent of its value when the lead content of the soil in the inhabited area surpasses the threshold of 1,000 ppm (parts per million) and 6 per cent when the corresponding figure is between 500 and 1,000 ppm.[36] So there tends to be a relation between pollution and property prices.

Postcolonialism and environmental crisis: the conflict in Darfur

Without doubt, ecological inequalities in general and, in particular, environmental racism, take on their most acute form in the postcolonial context. In a column published in the *Washington Post* in June 2007 the UN general secretary Ban Ki Moon stated that the fighting in Darfur was linked to climatic pressures: 'It is no accident', he declared, 'that the violence in Darfur erupted during the drought.'[37] Like all postcolonial conflicts, this war resulted from numerous inter-twined factors, but Ban Ki Moon was at least right to say that the ecology of the conflict is of decisive importance for understanding how it broke out and then went on to unfold. More precisely, we could say that political ecology provides the most adequate viewpoint for understanding the dynamic of the factors involved.

In recent years, the war in Darfur has been the object of a public awareness campaign such as few African conflicts have previously enjoyed. An international coalition called Save Darfur,[38] bringing together dozens of churches and other organizations, has since 2004 campaigned for an end to the 'genocide' and for intervention by the international community. Co-founded by public figures like Elie Wiesel and the ineffable George Clooney, the coalition's French branch includes supporters such as Bernard-Henri Lévy, Patrick Poivre d'Arvor and Bernard Kouchner. This conflict is usually presented as one opposing 'Arabs' to 'Africans', with the former portrayed as Muslims having come from the North or from outside the country who commit the bulk of the abuses, as against the 'Africans' native to this region of Western Sudan covering approximately one-fifth of the country's territory. The dividing line between the two groups is therefore essentially perceived as being ethnic and religious in character.

The reality could hardly be more different from this media representation. In fact most of the protagonists in this conflict are Muslims and all have the same skin colour.[39] To put that more pointedly, it is impossible to distinguish between two 'ethnic groups' on the basis of these criteria. Even just twenty years ago the very idea of 'Arabs' and 'Africans' would have been incomprehensible to the inhabitants of Darfur. The per-ception of this war in Western countries since it broke out in 2003 – or more accurately, since it became more aggravated; in fact there had already been conflicts before this date, par-ticularly in 1987–89 – is very much over-determined by the 'global war on terror' that has been underway since the 11 September 2001 attacks.[40] The war on terror has imposed a certain interpretative framework on all conflicts in the region, founded on categories like 'Muslims', 'Arabs', 'Islamists', 'terrorists' and so on. In this global war, the Khartoum government – held responsible for this situation – is a designated enemy of Washington; and President Omar al-Bashir does evidently bear some responsibility for the massacres and, in particular, for arming the Janjawid militias. Yet the conflict resists these interpretative assumptions: and in any case, not all the Janjawid are 'Arabs' and it is far from the case that all the 'Arabs' belong to these militias.[41]

Darfur is made up of different clans. Some of them are nomads while others are settled, and this distinction is crucial for understanding the social structure of this region. For a long time the coexistence of these two groups took place without major clashes, with the settled farmers of the Fur clan (Darfur means 'House of the Fur' in Arabic, with the Fur being the region's main ethnic group) allowing the nomads and, in particular, the Baggara tribe, to graze livestock on their land. However, starting in the 1970s, a series of extreme climatic phenomena upset the existing arrangements. The Sahel now fell victim to terrible droughts, in particular between 1982 and 1985. Deforestation accelerated, with 600,000 hectares of forest lost each year between 1990 and 2000.[42] Desertification, the erosion of the soil and sharply declining rainfall led to reduced agricultural production. At the same time as water became more scarce, the population of Darfur increased, from 1.1 million inhabitants in 1956 to 7.5 million in 2008.[43]

These climatic phenomena are forcing the groups on the ground to adapt, in a context in which resources are becoming increasingly scarce. The forests and pasture-lands accessible to the nomads are shrinking; all the more so given that the farmers, who are themselves under pressure, are now hostile to giving them access to their properties. This in turn drives the nomads to take up permanent abodes. The tensions over ever-less productive land multiply. And we can understand what follows from this.

Extra-environmental factors have also radicalized the conflict. Like the east and south of Sudan, Darfur is a historically poor region that has long been denied a share in the country's power and wealth, which are principally concentrated around Khartoum. Add to this the fact that numerous conflicts during the Cold War made weapons readily available in Africa, thus allowing the warring forces to arm themselves. Moreover, Darfur shares a border with Chad, a country that has been in an almost constant state of civil war since the 1960s and which also fought a foreign war with Gaddafi's Libya. Indeed, Gaddafi initially trained and armed the Janjawid militias.[44]

The result was a conflict that led to between 300,000 and 500,000 deaths, as well as 2.5 million refugees. Some estimates set the number of fatalities lower, at around 150,000. Whatever the case may be, military violence proper is responsible for only 25 per cent of these deaths, with the illness and malnutrition resulting from population displacements and the current living conditions accounting for the remainder of the total.[45]

These numbers do not alone explain the attention that this war has garnered in Western countries. By comparison, the war in the Democratic Republic of Congo claimed some five million victims from 1990 onward (all different causes of death included), without this stirring George Clooney to action. Women particularly fell victim to the violence in Darfur – as is often the case in the context of the 'new wars' that we discuss in Chapter 3. In the sexual division of labour that currently exists in the region, women are responsible for procuring water; but with desertification and declining rainfall, they have to travel ever greater distances to get to it, which makes them all the more exposed to violence from men.[46] It is very often the case that men cannot leave the refugee camps, for fear of being considered combatants and killed – and as such, women are effectively compelled to take on an increasing share of these responsibilities.

The people whom the Western media call 'Arabs' are most often former nomads, while 'Africans' refers to the settled tribes. The Muslim presence in the region goes back to the eighth century – that is, the very first decades of Islam's expansion. The idea that the Darfur conflict is the result of outsider Muslim Arabs' intrusion into a region that had up till then remained ethno-religiously 'pure' is therefore a false one.

Of course, there could be no question of arguing that the 'ethnic' dimension of the conflict is purely a media invention. Ethnic groups certainly do exist in Darfur, and for a simple reason: the British colonizers invented them. There was a sultanate in Darfur from the mid seventeenth century onward, but in the late nineteenth and early twentieth century the British took possession of the region, with the colonial period in Sudan lasting from 1916 to 1956. The incoming British established a system of land property rights, attributing portions of land to certain ethnicities and not others.[47] On the one hand, this system allowed them to control the local populations, after the tribes of Darfur had determinedly opposed British conquest. Moreover, it allowed the British to profit from the region economically, particularly by way of taxation. An early crystallization of these 'ethnic groups' took place on the basis of landed property (and, therefore, on a class basis), as British colonialism gave rise to an opposition between the settlers and the nomads, with those who were attributed land henceforth being opposed to the others. The current conflict is the ultimate result of this property system. Such approaches were commonplace among imperialists at the time, in what Mahmood Mamdani has called the strategy of 're-define and rule'. Indeed, the opposition between the Hutus and the Tutsis in Rwanda has a similar genealogy.

The sociologist Harald Welzer has said that Darfur is one of those 'conflicts that have ecological causes' and yet 'are perceived as ethnic conflicts'.[48] As we have seen, this was also Ban Ki-moon's view, expressed in his *Washington Post* column in 2007. Given what we have observed thus far, we can say that they are simultaneously both correct and mistaken. They are wrong because ethnic groups are the object of a long history in Darfur, going back to the colonial period; and over time, this has made them into a reality. Their mode of existence is historical, and we have to understand this history if we are to grasp the current conflict. At the same time, however, they are also correct, insofar as over the last half-century this colonial and postcolonial history has collided with extreme climatic phenomena, which has led to an intensifying crystallization of ethnic identities.

Ecological inequalities: A Marxist approach

The various ecological inequalities – including environmental racism – all lead back to one simple idea: that capitalism simultaneously both presupposes and generates inequalities in both individuals' and groups of individuals' relationship with the environment. If, as Marx said, capital is a 'social relation', then this relation also integrates 'nature' or 'the environment' into its logic. In sum, the intersection of class, race and gender has to be completed by a fourth dimension – nature – that complicates this intersection at the same time as itself being complicated by these three other terms. The ordering and causal primacy of one – or some – of these logics is specific to each occasion. Sometimes ecological inequalities are mixed in with these other terms to the point that they are difficult to distinguish from them. In other cases, they explain other inequalities, like when what at first glance look like 'ethnic' inequalities are in reality underpinned by environmental ones. In still other cases, they aggravate logics of inequality that originate somewhere else. Under the capitalist system inequalities have a cumulative or self-reinforcing dimension, even if it is sometimes also the case that the encounter between two forms of inequality may open up spaces of individual freedom. In each and every circumstantial situation, the Marxist compass used in this study seeks out the traces or effects of the logic of capital and the class struggle and thus accords an in-principle primacy to this factor. But this logic takes on singular forms that depend on each situation.

If nature appears to be 'universal' and to stand outside of social relations, we should then question the way in which it is *produced* in the modern age, in the sense that Henri Lefebvre spoke of a 'production of space'[49] – in this case, natural space. The 'great divide' between nature and culture has been the object of numerous works over recent decades, particularly those resulting from a 'constructivist'-minded anthropology of the sciences.[50] Bruno Latour has made it a particular speciality of his work to demonstrate the 'constructed' character of this 'great divide', within the perspective of a general theory of (non-)modernity. However, fundamentally this is a theory with very little politics to it, even if it is expounded in books with titles like *Politics of Nature* and *Les Atmosphères de la politique*, or journals like *Cosmopolitiques*.[51]

The 'pragmatist' epistemology that most of these works start out from is also inadequate to giving account of the systemic and conflictive character of environmental inequalities. What political purpose does the great divide between nature and culture serve? How is it connected to the logic of capital, the class struggle, or the form of the modern state? In what measure have imperialism and colonialism influenced this process? In vain would we search for answers to these questions in Bruno Latour's works. To address these problems in a Marxist manner, as we are doing here, requires that we 'plug them into' a theory of capitalism and its effects in all spheres of society.

Taking a closer look, we can see that there are various different sorts of environmental inequalities.[52] A first kind is the one that manifested itself in Warren County and South Central, where different sections of the population were unequally affected by the harmful consequences of the industrial process. All other things being equal, being poor, Black, or a woman – or all three at once – is an index of how much you will suffer the effects of such cases. Toxic waste is an example of this type of effect, but there are also others, like air pollution or lead poisoning among the children of immigrants. The subaltern classes are not always and everywhere the primary victims of all environmental problems, and that is why our formulation includes the caveat 'all other things being equal'. For example, automobile traffic and its consequences for air quality particularly affect city centres, and these are areas where a significant portion of the bourgeoisies of Europe live.[53] City centres also tend to be less well supplied with green spaces than certain suburbs are. However, the logic of the system implies that the popular classes are the main victims of these problems.

We also find ecological inequalities in access to the resources that nature offers, whether 'raw' ones or those that involve technical processes. These resources can be broken down into two different types. Firstly, there are 'elementary' natural assets, like water or energy sources: wood, coal, oil . . . this is what some have called 'environmental public services'.[54] They are more or less public and/or private according to the era and the country concerned, and the importance of each of these natural resources also varies over time.

Inequalities in water access have a very long history. However, they have become increasingly visible again since the last third of the twentieth century, on account of neoliberal policies privatizing the production and distribution of water. The revolt in Cochabamba, Bolivia, at the start of the 2000s, as well as the water wars in Latin America more generally, are examples of the conflicts to which these policies have led.[55]

These inequalities in water access also exist in France. In Guyana 15 per cent of the population does not have access to drinking water and, in certain regions, this figure reaches close to 50 per cent.[56] We can note analogous unequal situations in both electricity and waste disposal.[57] (Not to mention the natural risks to which the French West Indies, for example, are exposed, from earthquakes to volcanoes, cyclones, flooding and landslides. The West Indies are classed as a Level 3 seismic zone, which requires the construction of earthquake-proofed infrastructure – and yet this is not put into practice, on account of the costs that it would engender.)[58]

As for metropolitan France, not all territories have water of the same quality, or with a comparable relation between quality and price. A recent study thus showed that more than two million people consume water with excessive pollutant levels (pesticides, nitrates, selenium), in particular in agricultural regions.[59]

Energy poverty is another form of inequality in access to resources. It is defined by a lack of means for heating, or by the abnormal toxicity of the combustibles and the fittings used for heating, which increases the risk of accidents.[60] Today, Greece is a textbook example of energy poverty. In Athens it costs €1,000 a year to heat an averagely-sized apartment with gas; it takes only €250 to do so with wood.[61] The impoverishment of the population on account of the crisis has led numerous Greeks to choose this second option, which has in turn led to a sharp increase in illegal tree-felling and accelerated deforestation. Moreover, given the austerity measures that are supposedly meant to sort out the country's finances, the number of forest guards has been reduced, further encouraging illegal tree-felling. The European Union's Directorate-General for the Environment – that is, the same EU that is imposing these austerity measures on the Greeks – has become alarmed by this accelerated deforestation and has called on the Greek government to take the necessary measures in response.[62] It is estimated that air pollution in Athens has grown by close to 17 per cent since the beginning of the crisis, precisely as a result of the increased use of wood for heating. The economic crisis has thus become an ecological one – and vice versa. During 2012 in France, 230,000 households saw their electricity or gas supply cut off because they could not pay their bills – 20 per cent more than in 2011.[63]

Beyond basic natural assets, we also ought to take into consideration 'secondary' ones, from natural parks to landscapes, lakes, forests . . . in sum, what we call 'amenities'. Access to these, too, is distributed unequally across the population. Evidently, not all amenities are located in rich neighbourhoods and working-class districts are sometimes situated close to a forest or a lake. One such example is the La Coudraie *cité* [housing estate, similar to US 'projects'] in Poissy (Yvelines), in the Paris suburbs, one among the *cités* in the region facing great difficulties.[64] The degradation of the built environment and the social problems there led the authorities to launch an urban renovation plan, which envisaged that 500 homes be demolished and their inhabitants rehoused. In France, there is a well-established tradition of treating social problems as questions of urban planning. However, the residents, who were attached to their neighbourhood and thus opposed to the renovation plan, organized themselves and mounted an effective challenge to the proposals, thus succeeding in preventing the demolition of the estate. And one of the factors that explains the inhabitants' attachment to their estate, when it was put into question, was the proximity of the Poissy forest. This is an amenity integrated into the structure of their everyday lives and a reason to valorize the space in which they live.

Even so, it is clear that the presence of amenities is correlated with socio-economic factors. An INSEE investigation into housing, carried out at the beginning of the 2000s, thus showed that only 36 per cent of the inhabitants of *Zones urbaines sensibles* have a positive opinion of the green spaces available to them – only half as much as the rest of the population. There is a simple explanation for this: the number and quality of these spaces are linked to the state of a *commune*'s or a region's public finances.[65] The richer a *commune* is, the more money it can devote to the construction or maintenance of green spaces. Moreover, the presence of this type of space tends to push up property prices and to exclude poor households. Here, too, therefore, the logic of the market produces environmental exclusion effects.

There are also ecological inequalities in populations' exposure to 'risk', be it natural or industrial in character: an explosion at a chemicals plant, a dam bursting, flooding, the dissemination of GM seeds, earth tremors, epidemics . . .[66] One example of the unequal distribution of natural risks was the 2003 heatwave. This led to 15,000 excess deaths in France, more than 2,000 of them on 12 August 2003 alone. *The Institut national de veille sanitaire* (INVS; National Health Surveillance Institute) has established that age was one of the key variables for determining who the victims of this heatwave were – with the least self-sufficient elderly people being particularly badly affected – while the most important such variable was socio-economic category. This is what an INVS report had to say on the matter:

> the working-class [*ouvrier*] category seems still to be the one most at risk. This link between professional category and the risk of death could be due to persons' different sensitivity to risk, in function of their working careers. It could also be due to the inequalities among persons when faced with risk, on account of their different economic conditions. For example, the question of socio-professional category is linked to the number of rooms in the home . . . and we might suppose that people occupying large homes were more easily able to protect themselves by choosing the room least exposed to the heat.[67]

We could also hypothesize that the proximity of hospitals and doctors, or people's better or worse health – a variable that is closely correlated to socio-professional category – had an impact on the mortality rate.

The differing environmental 'footprints' that different population categories make are also a form of ecological inequality. To put that another way, it makes almost no sense to speak of the impact that society in general has on the environment. Studies looking into this question show that the footprint that people make is related to their income, as judged by various different yardsticks. Thus the European households that have the least impact on the environment are most often low-income single-adult households (with or without children), with the main householder being economically inactive and likely either relatively young (under thirty) or elderly (over sixty years of age).[68] Conversely, higher-income households have a greater negative impact on the environment. Even so, the evidence from certain data demands that we place certain caveats on this conclusion. For example, in the Paris region workers are the population category that covers the greatest distance in motorized journeys, of the order of 7.4 kilometres per trip, which is more than the middle and upper classes.[69] This is explained by the fact that they generally live further from their workplaces, given their lower incomes and the lower property prices in peripheral areas. This does not at all deny that environmental inequalities do exist, but it demonstrates that they are complicated by other types of inequalities.

The September 2001 explosion at the AZF factory shows that it is principally the working classes who are affected by industrial hazards. This catastrophe led to thirty deaths and left thousands injured. As many as 27,000 homes were affected by the explosion, more than 15,000 of them in the HLMs.[70] After the explosion, the city's most prominent buildings, like the Palais des Sports and the Stadium – where Toulouse Football Club plays each week – were quickly rebuilt. However, the working-class neighbourhoods adjacent to the factory had to wait several days for help to arrive and long months before the insurance companies paid out for the damage. This gave rise – particularly in the working-class Le Mirail neighbourhood – to the mobilization of the *sans fenêtres*: people whose windows had been shattered by the explosion but had not had anyone sent to replace them, or who would only belatedly benefit from repair operations. This movement displayed a very considerable family resemblance with the movement for environmental justice.

The absence of so-called 'ethnicity' statistics in France prevents us determining exactly who the victims of the factory explosion were, or who participated in the *sans fenêtres* movement. Nonetheless, data collected on the ground allow us to get some measure of the environmental racism at work in this area. For example, in a *sans fenêtres* petition addressed to the mayor's office by seventy Le Mirail tenants, more than half of the names are Arab-sounding.[71] Indeed, social and racial inequalities have long been building up in Toulouse. In the 1920s a chemicals plant was set up in the south-west of the city.[72] Over the decades the space between the centre of the city and this facility was filled up with housing and new residents, including an immigrant workforce of largely North African origin. The Le Mirail neighbourhood was built in the 1960s, immediately adjacent to this plant. Meanwhile the bourgeois neighbourhoods are separated from it by natural parks. The AZF explosion was thus a kind of résumé of the city's industrial and migration histories.

This situation is not specific to Toulouse alone. In France there are 670 industrial sites classed under the Seveso Directive.[73] Most of them are located near working-class neighbourhoods, for the simple reason that property prices are lower in these areas. A 2003 law made it compulsory to implement 'Plans to Prevent Technological Risks', which are supposed to reduce the risks of industrial catastrophe and to make inhabitations more resistant in case of explosion. However, this law was only weakly implemented, also because the inhabitants themselves would have had to pay for part of the building consolidation costs. These residents are thus literally prisoners of these neighbourhoods: they neither have the financial resources necessary to leave; nor do they have the means to protect themselves from a possible future catastrophe.

The archaeology of environmental racism

Explaining the persistence of environmental racism in the contemporary social world demands that we set it in a historical, long-term perspective. In the modern era, the inextricable link between race and nature emerged in a particular ecosystem: the slave plantation. The plantation is a total social fact that leaves no sphere untouched; and nature is itself captured by the logic of the plantation, whose end goal is, after all, to draw profits from it.

> Direct slavery is just as much the pivot of bourgeois industry as machinery, credits, etc. Without slavery you have no cotton;

without cotton you have no modern industry. It is slavery that gave the colonies their value; it is the colonies that created world trade, and it is world trade that is the precondition of large-scale industry. Thus slavery is an economic category of the greatest importance.[74]

Slavery is not a phenomenon from another age, that the logic of capital definitively transcended. Rather, it is one of the matrixes of the industrial civilization within which our development today takes place. As such, the type of social relations that emerged within the plantation still condition present-day societies.

In the plantation context, the master–slave dialectic transforms into a master–slave–nature dialectic.[75] For example, cotton-growing involves various different things being set in relation: the cotton fibre itself, but also water, earth, sunlight, a racist social system and ideology, technologies of constraint (the master's whip), a legal framework . . . and at the heart of this symbiotic relationship, we find the slave's labour. The slave realizes the synthesis or the mediation of these different elements and sets them in motion through her labour. That is the reason why in the nineteenth-century US South slaves constituted the most important form of property, in terms of their financial value. The average (mean) price of a slave rose from 300 dollars in 1810 to 800 dollars in 1860, with the total value of the country's slaves reaching close to four billion dollars, more than the value of livestock or real estate in that period.[76] Moreover, the plantation was plugged into international markets, in particular the textile markets, as they continued to expand across the nineteenth century.

Depending on circumstances, the master–slave–nature dialectic turns to the advantage of one or the other of the antagonists. The master, of course, seeks to draw the greatest possible profit from his human and natural possessions. Nonetheless, this is a difficult objective to fulfil, due to cotton's own intrinsic characteristics. Until very late on, cotton was picked by hand, as mechanized harvesting did not produce the desired results. In these conditions, the master's only way to increase the amount of cotton picked was either the ever-more intensive exploitation of slaves or (through purchase or reproduction) an increase in their overall number.

Cotton's natural properties thus confer a particular form on its production and on the struggle that it plays theatre to.

The slaveowner's efforts to intensify exploitation also ran up against another natural limit: the slave's body and its capacities of endurance. This body can be brutalized, but only up to a certain point. At the very least, the body needs nourishment and rest. In order to draw as much out of the body as possible, but without breaking it, the master is forced to make concessions. That is why slaves were sometimes given permission to grow a vegetable patch, allowing them to improve their everyday diet.[77] These gardens let them escape the master's grip for a time, or even to escape entirely, since the patches concerned were often situated on the boundaries between the plantation and the forest – and we can add to that the fact that the slaves most often went there at night, given that their days were devoted to picking cotton. The natural limits to exploitation thus open up spaces of freedom for its victims.

The alliance between cotton – that is, nature – and the slaves also took on other forms. Various threats hung over cotton growing, from bacteria to insects, weather and so on. When such calamities occurred they interrupted the cycle of production, allowing the slaves some breathing space. The control of slave women's wombs was also crucial for the plantation owner, since as we have seen reproduction is a means of increasing the workforce and thus production itself. These women's refusal to procreate thus constituted an act of resistance – a refusal to bring into the world beings who would live as slaves.[78] Moreover, as it happens, one chance outcome of natural selection is the fact that cotton contains gossypol, a molecule that reduces fertility when it is chewed. Slaves were the custodians of sophisticated medicinal knowledges, partly imported from Africa and transmitted from generation to generation, and they used them as part of their strategy of resistance against oppression.[79]

The ecology of the plantation has left a footprint on the structuring of space in the US South and other regions of the world where slavery existed. When the South began to industrialize at the end of the nineteenth century, polluting industries were often established on the sites of former plantations, around which a majority Black population lived. One of the best known of these regions, situated in Louisiana, runs from Baton Rouge to New Orleans and is known as 'chemical corridor' or 'cancer alley'. This corridor has a higher than average percentage of cancers and other afflictions, and the presence of these polluting industries is a major reason for this.[80] Things have come full circle: a process that began with the exploitation of the slaves' labour continues with the exploitation of their descendants' health. In the same register, in today's China we see that the Chinese themselves use the term 'cancer villages' to refer to those locations where populations' health is endangered by abnormally high pollution levels linked to the country's industrial development.[81] (In this case it does not seem that the victim is any particular ethnic group, as this phenomenon affects the peasantry in a more indiscriminate manner).

Blacks are not the only victims of environmental racism in the United States. Native Americans are the object of a specific environmental racism whose genealogy partly differs from that which Blacks suffer. In 1830, under Andrew Jackson's presidency, the US Congress passed the *Indian Removal Act*, ordering the deportation of the Native Americans from their lands of origin towards the West, beyond the Mississippi. Ten years later, there were practically none of them left to the east of this frontier. Not only were the Native Americans expelled from their lands of origin, but the reserves in which they lived increasingly tended to be situated in the surroundings of military zones. With the United States's rise as an economic and military power, the US armed forces needed sites where they could exercise their troops, but also for testing weapons and in particular – from the 1940s onward – nuclear ones.

A nuclear colonialism was thus put in place, with military-nuclear complexes now being located close to the territories occupied by Native Americans, notably including the largest such complex in Nevada.[82] Successive administrations in Washington did what they could to spare White populations such nuisances. A systematic study of the location of these complexes across the country leaves no room for doubt: the higher the area in m^2 occupied by Native Americans in any given region, the greater the probability that we will find military installations there.[83]

Race and reforestation

In the nineteenth century, France was also the site of a social and colonial construction of nature. In Chapter 3 we will see that the control of forest resources has been a crucial military question ever since the beginning of the modern era. This control developed through the implementation of a policy that built a genuine 'dam' holding back the peasantry and its free access to resources. Yet this is not only a military matter, but also an economic one. Effectively, it is a question of transforming natural resources into private property; or, to put that another way, commodifying them. The commodification of nature that we can see today is but the latest in a long series of such waves of privatization, beginning with the English enclosures of the seventeenth century. In 1842 Karl Marx published a succession of articles in the *Rheinische Zeitung* devoted to 'the theft of wood'.[84] These texts were written in response to a debate over the regulation of access to forests, which was then taking place in the Rhineland *Diet* [parliament]. The authorities wanted to put an end to the illegal appropriation of these resources. As Daniel Bensaïd remarked in his brilliant preface to these articles of Marx's, 'the stakes that were coming into profile, behind the *Diet*'s debate on the theft of wood' were 'the modern distinction between private and public and its application to property rights. The significant quantity of wood thefts – as the judicial statistics of the time demonstrate – illustrate simultaneously both the survival of customary practices of usage rights and the growing criminalization of these practices by the capitalist society coming into formation.' The question of nature and its usages is thus to be found at the heart of the modern construction of the private and the public – that is to say, the consolidation of capitalist property.

This construction is the object of a merciless struggle among different social classes. The peasants did not hesitate to challenge the state-implemented containment policy. In 1829 the 'War of the *Demoiselles* [maidens]' took place in Ariège; a peasant rebellion that targeted the landowners and the forest guards. This revolt owes its name to the fact that the peasants disguised themselves as women in order to catch their adversaries by surprise. More generally, the 1830s and 1840s were the theatre of recurrent violent attacks against the forest guards. This was particularly the case during the revolution of 1848, though this dimension of the revolution is often passed over in silence.[85] The forest guards were the symbol of the 'growing criminalization' of the usage of the forests, as described by Daniel Bensaïd. So one first front of the appropriation of natural resources split mainland France itself. It would set the terms of a confrontation between the subaltern classes – with the peasantry in the lead – and, on the other hand, the landowners and the state.

Conversely, a second front separated the metropole from the colonies. In mainland France, nature became more and more positively connotated over the nineteenth century. The forests incarnated France's collective memory, which connected the present day back to glorious past eras of her national history.[86] In this sense, the forests are a constituent part of France's history. The notion of 'heritage' emerged in this era, applying to nature as well as to cultural artefacts. In these times of revolutionary troubles beginning at the end of the eighteenth century, forests constituted a haven of stability; though that did not of course prevent them also being exploited for economic or military purposes. That is why it was necessary to do everything possible to preserve them.

Forests in the colonies were also a focus of conservation policies, albeit for different reasons. As the agronomist François Trottier wrote in the quotation heading this chapter, taken from an 1876 work tellingly entitled *Reforestation and Colonisation*: 'Reforestation is the means by which our race will conserve its European faculties.' The degradation of nature was perceived as a threat to (European) civilization; not only because it was a resource that it was possible to draw a profit from, but because given that environment is character-forming, its deterioration would necessarily lead to a weakened character. Some have spoken, in this regard, of a *climatic orientalism*:[87] the superiority of the European races being linked, among other things, to their capacity to take care of their environment. The environment supposedly exercised a positive influence on the European races' character; conversely, the 'oriental' populations left the environment to degradation and this was held to be simultaneously both a symptom and a cause of their own degeneration. In these conditions, it was necessary to do everything to ensure that the Europeans settling in Africa or Asia would not also succumb to this degraded nature. In the second half of the nineteenth century, organizations similar to the US Group of Ten mentioned above also began appearing in France. The *Club alpin* was created in 1872, the *Touring Club* in 1890 and the *Société pour la protection des paysages* [Landscapes Protection Society] in 1901. For its part, the *Ligue pour le reboisement de l'Algérie* [League for the Reforestation of Algeria] was founded in 1882. These organizations played an important role in turning nature into national heritage; that is, in defining a *patriotic concern for nature*. The *Club alpin*, for example, explicitly linked love for the mountains and *amor patria*. It also maintained close relations with the French army. In the final decades of the nineteenth century its officials thus called on the army to form units of skier-soldiers in order to ensure the security of mountainous border areas.[88] The objective was not only to secure the Alpine space, but also to encourage the population to get better acquainted with it, given the mountains' virtues in regenerating the human character. The history of skiing in France is a military history.

Purifying nature . . .

Modern nature is opposed to the modern city in every respect.[89] Since the second half of the nineteenth century, it has been the site where the White middle and upper classes have come to take refuge from the sound and fury of the metropolises. The main beneficiaries of capitalist civilization are the same people who have the means to escape from it. That said, nature has not, of course, always been positively connoted – far from it. For a long time it was considered the opposite of civilization, as a site of savagery that inspired terror. Over the nineteenth century, however, the valences of nature and culture, rural and the urban, were gradually reversed. The Romantic movement, whose exponents sacralized nature, was simultaneously both a cause and a consequence of this inversion. As Theodor Adorno put it in his essay 'On Lyric Poetry and Society', this sacralization of nature was conceivable only in a context in which the individual feels more and more alienated from the evolutions of society itself. In this sense, social alienation and the valorization of nature are two concomitant processes.[90] More precisely, Adorno's argument is that nature's prestige rises in periods of political defeat and normalization, like under the July Monarchy, when the affects invested in the revolutionary transformation of society are disappointed.

The growing strength of ecologist parties and the ecologist movement from the second half of the 1970s onward, at the moment when the propulsive force of May 1968 was exhausted, could perhaps be explained by this same phenomenon. Even so, in certain countries, at least, this movement emerged at the same time as the movements of the 1960s and 1970s and not after their decline.[91] Rachel Carson's *Silent Spring* was a bestseller as early as 1962; while the slogan 'Give Earth a chance' was a direct spin-off of 'Give peace a chance'. A movement as complex as the ecologist movement is necessarily the product of multiple and discordant processes.

The aesthetic of the sublime, whose modern form was established by Edmund Burke and by Kant, contributes to this tendency to sacralize nature. It is no chance thing that Burke had been the first and the most intelligent of the opponents of the French Revolution. Modern political revolutions, just like the industrial revolution, essentially unfold in the urban space; the 'acceleration' of the temporalities characteristic of modern life takes place in cities.[92] Burke's conservatism was the other side of the coin to this process and in his *Reflections on the Revolution in France* he counterposed such acceleration to the constancy of the institutions of the *ancien régime*, which had passed 'the test of time'. In this context, nature gradually became a haven of stability – the inverse reflection of the civilization of capital. In this sense, it is also a pure product of this civilization. Finding in nature a moment of escape from the alienation of the modern world, the bourgeois and/or aristocrat (depending on the country) thus found a form of authenticity. Of course, that is not to say that nature was always and everywhere positively connoted in the nineteenth century – far from it. We need only think of

Baudelaire's disdain for nature in his *Peintre de la vie moderne* (1863) and his celebration of the artificial. But this quest for authenticity did, in this era, gradually become a 'class experience' – to adopt a term that E. P. Thompson employed with regard to a different theme – and it was combined with a certain representation of nature. The people likely to have such an experience were those who had access to nature – in other words, those who had the time and means necessary for accessing it – while those who continually had to sell their labour power in order to live were excluded from it.

With economic development and the growth of the middle classes, in particular during the *Trente Glorieuses* [three decades of growth, post Second World War], this class experience became accessible to a growing number of individuals, albeit doubtless in altered form. Nature was democratized. Families now acquired a car or two, allowing them to head out to natural parks and the mountains. The 'consumer society' appearing at this moment also included the consumption of nature. Indeed, the economist John Kenneth Galbraith noted this link between mounting consumerism and nature as early as 1958.[93] Yet a significant part of the population remained excluded from this democratization, even after the *Trente Glorieuses*. For the poorest and the less White, the environment is at best an abstract notion and at worst an argument employed by the public powers to divert attention from their own problems. As Carl Stokes, 1968–71 mayor of Cleveland and first Black mayor of any major American city explained, 'The nation's concern with environment has done what George Wallace was unable to do: distract the nation from the human problems of Black and Brown Americans' (George Wallace was an Alabama Democrat and staunch defender of racial segregation).[94] The idea that 'environmental' problems (narrowly defined) are opposed to the demands of ethnic minorities and the workers' movement was deeply anchored in this period – just as it is, in many aspects, even today.

. . . and naturalizing race

If nature was the object of class, gender and racial definitions in the nineteenth and twentieth centuries, it in turn contributed to constructing and consolidating these other categories. In other words, race, class, gender and nature were the objects of a co-construction taking place in the modern epoch. The nineteenth-century emergence of 'wilderness' was inextricably linked to the historically concomitant emergence of 'Whiteness'.[95] The city was dark and dirty and that was where the dark and dirty individuals *par excellence* were to be found: Blacks, immigrants (Irish, Italians, Poles) and workers – these in fact often being the same people. In his environmental history of the United States, Mark Fiege delves into the urban history of Topeka, the capital city of Kansas.[96] Topeka was important to the emergence of the civil rights movement, since the 1954 Supreme Court ruling on *Brown vs. Board of Education*, putting an end to racial segregation in schooling, in fact revolved around this city's schools.

The Black neighbourhoods of Topeka have systematically been located in the lower part of town, in flood zones. The richer districts, conversely, are mostly situated on the heights of the city. In the first decades of the twentieth century, 60 per cent of flood victims were Black, a phenomenon that we could also observe in New Orleans a century later, with the onset of Hurricane Katrina. Moreover, today we can see the same thing across the 'planet of slums'.[97] The names of the Black neighbourhoods of Topeka thus evoke Blackness, dirtiness or lowliness: they are called Mudtown or Bottoms. In the representations that were most widespread in this era, there were frequent comparisons between these areas and the character and aspect of the persons who lived there. The end of the nineteenth and the beginning of the twentieth century corresponded to the birth of the social sciences, ever more strongly emphasizing the degree to which individuals were influenced by the environment, including in the thinking of theorists of Black liberation like WEB Du Bois.[98]

Whiteness is the antonym of this dirtiness and darkness and is synonymous with purity.[99] This purity characterizes not only the White ruling classes and their neighbourhoods, but also nature, which is their privileged space. As Sierra Club founder John Muir put it, 'nothing truly wild is unclean', since impurity is an evil born to civilization, in the cities. Muir did not, of course, himself come up with such an idea. We find it a century earlier in Rousseau, albeit in different form.[100] What was different, when Muir said it, was that given the growth in the power of racial categories across the nineteenth century – in the United States, but also more generally – this idea entered into interaction with a racialized political and economic system and indeed took root therein. Wilderness and Whiteness are thus two categories – or more precisely, two *institutions* – that mutually reinforce one another.

US nature was only 'pure' to the extent that Native Americans, the dirty and dark group *par excellence*, were displaced from it. They along with Blacks (at the same time, but according to different modalities) were the great outcasts of the 'nature' being constructed in this era. This exclusion, which proceeded by way of both massacres and the displacement of Native American populations into preservation, was a condition of White middle- and upper-class tourists being able to experience the authenticity of the rivers, canyons, forests, mountains, wild animals, etc. As Carolyn Merchant has noted, there is, then, an *environmental history of race*; that is to say, Whiteness and the experience of the self that goes with it are defined in terms of the environment.[101]

This environmental history of race relates to gender in a rather complex way. Certain present-day feminist epistemologies are keen to establish an analogy between man's domination of woman and man's domination of nature. From this point of view, economic development as well as scientific knowledge are possible thanks to the subjection of nature – in the dual sense of 'dominating it' and in terms of 'making it a subject of investigation' – and the subjugation of women. On the economic terrain this subjugation translates into the exploitation of women in the family home and, in the scientific domain, the exclusion of (supposedly) 'feminine' forms of knowledges from legitimate scientific understanding.

Nature complicates the 'mutual engendering' of racial and sexual categories, relations that have existed since the eighteenth century.[102] As Elsa Dorlin has shown, the relation between these categories is, in one aspect, a relation of analogy, in that their co-construction operates by way of approximation and differentiation. But it is also a historical relation, as racial categories are in part derived from sexual categories, hence the idea (which gives Dorlin's work its title) of a 'Womb of Race'.[103] The differentiation between the sexes was thus one of the criteria making it possible to establish a hierarchy of races at the threshold of the modern era. If Africans were considered an inferior race, this was because African men are beardless, that is, less differentiated from women of the same race. A more careful analysis should be able to demonstrate what aspects of the relation between nature and these other forms of categorization belong to the order of analogy or of derivation. That is not to say that the analysis would be the same for each country; we can be certain that the opposite is true. After all, this relation takes place within the terms of singular national histories and state mechanisms.

Exporting the environment

Across the whole twentieth century, Western imperialists exported nature and the class experience that is inextricably linked to it. Organizations like the World Wildlife Fund (WWF, founded in the 1960s) spread the American model of national parks in more or less close alliance with the elites of the countries concerned, notably in Africa and Asia. These natural parks have often been established without regard for local populations, most often poor ones lacking in political influence. The Indian historian Ramachanda Guha thus recalls how the 1970s 'Tiger Project', advocating the creation of reserves protecting the Bengal tiger, led to the displacement of a great number of villages and their inhabitants.[104] The process at work in Warren County is also apparent here, in other climes and in different terms: that is to say, the construction of an unspoilt nature and of the class experience that this makes possible – putting tigers on display, to be admired by Indian and international elites – supposes the dispossession of whole swathes of the population. It also implies the restriction of ecology to questions of preservation or conservation. Like the residents of Warren County or South Central, the populations of India are confronted with very far-reaching environmental problems: pollution, water and fuel poverty, the erosion of the soil, drought, etc. With climate change, these problems never stop building up. But they do not enter into the field of legitimate environmentalist concerns.

The implantation of this model is based on a long history of colonial ecology or 'ecological imperialism'.[105] The Kenyan case illustrates this. The British introduced nature conservation policies to this country in the late nineteenth century,[106] and from the beginning of the twentieth century they were backed by private imperial associations like the Society for the Preservation of the Wild Fauna of the Empire (later to become Fauna and Flora International). Such policies frequently entered into conflict with the interests of the local populations, for example in preventing the agricultural development of certain regions – to the detriment of their populations' wellbeing – in order to reserve vast territories for hunting or the safari. They imposed heavy fines for illegal attacks on wild animals, including when they threatened livestock or humans, and provided for little or no indemnification when herds were thus decimated. Moreover, these policies placed the usage of forests and land under the control of the colonial authorities. That is why they often gave rise to protests among the autochthonous populations.

During decolonization, international environmentalist organizations strained to make sure that these preservation policies were not put in question. The modernizing or 'developmentalist' economic policies often advocated by the regimes in newly independent countries led such bodies to fear that nature would be exploited in an uncontrolled manner. From the 1950s onward many international conferences were thus organized in Africa for the sake of convincing the elites that emerged from decolonization of the importance of nature preservation for tourism, or with a view to economic development. In this context, the prevalent attitude was a 'paternalist' one, with international organizations betting on these countries' incapacity to take care of their natural resources by themselves.

On the one hand, Westerners perceived the colonies – and later, the countries – of the Third World as the anti-wilderness *par excellence*. That is, they saw them as being subject to over-population, famines, civil war and environmental degradation. Conversely, when they are voided of their occupants, as in the case of natural parks, deserts, jungles and

other supposed 'virgin' spaces, these sites are positively connoted. This fallen nature contributes *a contrario* to the construction of nature in Western countries. If, as Edward Said
puts it, 'Orientalism is the Orient described by the West', in
the sense that in the nineteenth century the West constructed
itself in a fantasized and inverted relationship with the Orient,
then this orientalism also regards nature. For proof of this
we need only leaf through the pages of one of the main
vectors of this representation of 'oriental' nature in the West:
National Geographic magazine. As we see in a work by
feminist and postcolonial theorist Linda Steet analysing the
manner in which this publication has represented the Arab
world in photographs across the twentieth century, this is a
portrayal of *Veils and Daggers*.[107] Since its 1888 foundation,
the USA's *National Geographic* – one of the pedagogical tools
most used in the world's geography classrooms – has cease-
lessly essentialized the Orient, reducing it to an original and
unchangeable 'primitivism'.

The resources existing within the colonies – and then post-
colonies – were harnessed in the interests of the empires'
economic and military needs. Imperialism is predicated on an
awareness of the available resources, which explains its role
in producing new knowledges – in botany, geology, anthropology . . . – across the modern age. It also requires a capacity to plan the renewal and circulation of these resources,
particularly from the colonies towards the metropoles. As we
will see in Chapter 3, the management of wood, metal ores
and in particular water is of decisive military importance.
Hence the idea that some historians have advanced holding
that ecology – and even the modern concept of nature – has
one of its origins in colonization and, more precisely, in the
control of the colonized regions' nature.[108] This control
requires that these resources be taken out of the autochthonous peoples' hands, which explains the 'paternalist' dis-
courses claiming that they are incapable of taking care of
nature. It is here that ecological and cultural imperialisms
fuse. To take the case of the US empire, in the second half of
the twentieth century we can see the resurgence of powerful
neo-Malthusian currents of thinking, taking poor Americans
as well as Third-World populations as their object.[109] The
1968 publication of Paul Ehrlich's bestseller *The Population*

Bomb was one example of this. Such neo-Malthusianism was concomitant with the Cold War period, which saw the two superpowers clashing in proxy wars that took place in the Third World. In this context, control of natural resources was of decisive importance.

Ehrlich's book spoke not only of the poor populations of the global South, but equally those of the North. The neo-Malthusianism characteristic of large swathes of the 1960s environmentalist movement led to calls for drastic birth-rate controls; that is to say, as in Malthus's own thinking, controls on birth rates among the lowest social classes and minorities. This is one of the factors explaining the rupture between the environmental movement and the civil rights movement, which took hold right from the outset. Moreover, this period also saw a link being established between immigration and environmental degradation, with the struggle against immigration also being fought in the name of preserving the environment.[110] In neo-Malthusian perspectives, then, there is not (only) an opposition between an unspoilt nature in the centre and a degraded nature in peripheral regions. The corruption also spreads to the centre itself, in the sense that here we find populations whose birth rate and environmental impact the state must rigorously control.

The coming political ecology

If traditional environmentalist associations have difficulties recognizing the social dimension of ecology, the workers' movement has since its origins entertained an ambivalent relationship with environmental concerns. The aforementioned September 2001 explosion at the AZF factory brought to light a significant rupture between the trade unions and the associations representing those who were left displaced. On 21 March 2002, six months after the explosion, all the chemical workers' union federations staged a joint demonstration in Toulouse, in defence of the industry.[111] The lead banner declared 'The chemical industry is a necessity, safety a requirement.' The march's objective was to improve plant safety and defend employment in this sector, which was threatened by the measures taken by the authorities as well as the Total group (to which the factory belongs) following the catastrophe. The unions demanded that the undamaged parts of the factory be set working again, following the strengthening of safety measures. Workers from companies operating as the factory's subcontractors were also present at the demonstration.

Two days later, the 'Never again, here or anywhere' collective demonstrated in this same location. This collective brought together local residents and victims of the explosion as well as a number of associations, including environmental ones. Its objective was to have the factory shut down for good – in its eyes, the only way of guaranteeing the inhabitants' safety. It was revealed that even before the explosion Total had intended to close the factory due to its (real or supposed) lack of profitability. Opportunity makes the thief, or, as one commentator said in this regard, 'the explosion makes the thief'.[112] That is the reason why the unions saw an 'objective' alliance between the boss and these associations, with both of them having an interest in the factory closing, if for different reasons.

This split highlighted a division that structured the twentieth-century political terrain. That is, if it was the unions' responsibility to defend jobs and the industry providing them, sometimes to the exclusion of other concerns such as the safety of locals or even the workers themselves, it was left to the environmental associations and their allies to fight against pollution, industrial hazards and other harmful effects generated by economic production. Trade unionism has historically built itself on a belief in the beneficial effects of the development of the 'productive forces' and the positive consequences of such development for wage-earners' condition. In the French context, that is particularly true of the CGT. The period running from 1936 to 1945, from the Popular Front to the programme of the *Conseil national de la Résistance*, was decisive in forming the CGT's identity as a union.[113] In 1946, coming out of the war, the union devoted a report to reviving the country's productive apparatus, with a positive emphasis on the idea of 'subjugating nature' in service of this revival.[114] A 'productivist' reading of Marxism, very influential across the twentieth century – in particular due to its attachment to the Soviet model – also played a role in this. The creation of a rigid distinction between work and 'outside of work', was also decisively important, inducing a sharp split between, on the one hand, the unions, whose object was work and, on the other hand, 'associations', whose privileged domain was 'outside of work', or civil society – the underlying implication being that labour did not belong to this latter category.[115]

However, we should qualify this conclusion somewhat, since the link between trade unionism – and the workers' movement in general – and environmental questions is a complex one. First of all, in that wage-earners and their unions are perfectly conscious of industrial hazards. And with good reason: for they are on the front line when it comes to suffering the consequences. In a factory like AZF there can be major disasters like the one in September 2001, but also more 'ordinary' accidents: leakages, poisoning, fires, small explosions . . .[116] Indeed, such accidents occur frequently. If, as the work safety regulations prescribe, they led to production being interrupted on every occasion, then there would be constant starting and stopping. The consequence? The workers in these factories develop a sophisticated savoir-faire 'on the job', allowing them to handle these accidents in an 'informal' manner. Workers' creativity and courage are conditions of this type of plant's very functioning, just as in the industrial process in general. This often leads them to take what are major risks for their and their colleagues' health. Yet even if workplace health and safety is rarely recognized as an ecological problem in its own right, including by the mainstream ecology movement, it is just as much an ecological concern as the construction of an incinerator or the abnormally high noise in a working-class district neighbouring an airport.[117] A worker's health is the reflection or interface of her relationship with the environment, be it technical, natural, legal, or all three at once. As soon as we recognize this fact, the rupture between the trade-union and ecological domains already seems rather less sharp.

Moreover, in the 1960s the trade unions did become increasingly conscious of the importance of ecological issues. In France as elsewhere, this coming to awareness received an impulse from the social movements emphasizing these concerns. Even though large sections of the workers' movement were distrustful of ecologist movements, it was not systematically closed off to the ideas that they advanced, above all when they tallied with concerns relating to workplace hazards like the ones we have just mentioned. Trade unions gradually integrated certain ecological themes into their programme, particularly as mediated by the notion of people's 'living environment' [*cadre de vie*]. It seems that this notion first appeared in the trade-union press back in 1965, in the CFDT weekly *Syndicalisme Hebdo*,[118] and referred to everything to do with housing, transport, culture, the 'quality' or 'context' of people's lives, 'nuisances' (pollution, noise), etc. The 'living environment' was not just 'outside of work'.[119] Rather, it made it possible to think the connection between work and outside of work, to challenge the separation between them and not only to consider the individual in terms of the wage relation. In consequence, it implied a relative weakening of this distinction.

This notion of the 'living environment' was fed by a particularly dynamic theoretical output, for example the contributions by Michel de Certeau and André Gorz, or even the earlier works of Henri Lefebvre, with the first volume of his *Critique of Everyday Life* having come out at the end of the 1940s. The unions closest to the 'new social movements' such as the CFDT were not the only ones to take an interest in the 'living environment' and there were also debates on this question within the CGT from the early 1970s onward. It is interesting to note that this notion was principally discussed within the unions during the *Union de la Gauche*[120] period between 1972 and 1977 and in relation to this alliance's strategy. The *Union de la Gauche* drove the politicization of the unions, now abandoning any narrow division between a 'social' domain considered the unions' own remit and a 'political' terrain left to the parties. The 'desectionalization' – in Michel Dobry's terms – that we can see in the wake of May '68 would encourage the circulation of this type of thematic among different spheres of society.[121] The notion of 'environment' itself first appeared in CGT congress documents in 1972, albeit certainly endowed with a rather vague meaning.

It was not only ecologist movements that bore influence on the workers' movement with regard to environmental matters. Decolonization struggles had also contributed to the labour movement beginning to take ecological questions into consideration.[122] Already in the 1950s trade-union press we find denunciations of the pillage of the colonies' natural resources, notably in the Algerian case, while in a 1955 note to the *Conseil économique et social* one CFTC delegate lamented the deleterious effects of the French state's irrigation operations in terms of deforestation and eroding the soil. The exploitation of colonial populations and of nature were often denounced in conjunction, with the degradation of nature being presented as one of the causes of these peoples' poverty.

The hybridization of trade-union and environmental struggles has continued in recent years. There can be no doubt that the effectiveness of liberation movements in the twenty-first century will in large part depend on the deeper exploration of this hybridization. Within the context of its alliances with associations like AC! [Agir ensemble contre le chômage; Act together against unemployment] and APEIS [Association pour l'emploi, l'information et la solidarité des chômeurs et travailleurs précaires; Precarious and unemployed workers' association for employment, information and solidarity], since the early 2000s CGT Énergie has committed itself to 'Robin Hood' operations, consisting of re-connecting or refusing to cut off the current to private households denied electricity because they cannot pay their bills.[123] These operations are sometimes accompanied with cutting off the homes of bosses or elected representatives who support the privatization of EDF.

These actions principally took place during the mobilization against this privatization in 2004. Their objective was to demonstrate that the privatization of this company would lead to an increase in electricity prices, from which the poorest would suffer. This was a way of showing that this struggle was not a 'corporatist' movement only concerning the defence of EDF employees' status.

These 'Robin Hood' operations speak to the current resurgence of 'repertoires of action' dating back to before the emergence of the modern workers' movement in the second half of the nineteenth century. They were comparable to what Eric Hobsbawm classically called 'social banditry'.[124] They were about taking from the rich to give to the poor and to that end they based themselves on a 'moral' conception of social justice. EDF agents have always carried out this type of operations, but until now they were a matter of individual initiative, rather than something the union publicly took responsibility for.

These actions exhibited a very close affinity with the environmental justice movement, even if they were carried out within a trade-union context. As one CGT Énergie official explained 'there were neighbourhoods that we hadn't been able to go into any more because blue cars are synonymous with the power being cut off (the guys went in with fear in their stomachs – they had stones thrown at them), and now we went back in to these neighbourhoods, showing our faces'.[125] These 'Robin Hood' operations thus made it possible to tear down the frontier separating the trade union from the environmental domain and, in this case, from a question of energy. At the same time, they were an opportunity to establish links with sections of the population who are often foreign to trade-union action, in particular in working-class neighbourhoods, which are also areas where we find a large proportion of ethno-racial minorities. So among other things this was also a form of struggle against environmental racism. It is here that the future of political ecology is being played out, in the hybridization of struggles and the construction of unprecedented alliances.

Conclusion

Let's recap. Environmental inequalities constitute a structuring fact of political power relations in the modern era. They mean that the harmful consequences of capitalist development are not suffered in the same way or to the same degree by all sectors of the population. These inequalities long preceded the current ecological crisis. Yet as we shall see in a moment, this crisis does tend to aggravate them. One particular form of ecological inequality has held our attention, here, namely environmental racism. But to understand this latter requires that we also take into account other logics of inequality and, in particular, class and gender.

Starting from this basis, the whole question is to determine what are the means that capitalism uses to mortgage or manage the conflicts that result from ecological inequalities, in particular when they intensify on account of the environmental crisis. Capitalism generates crisis, but it also produces 'antibodies' to the crisis, which allow it to mortgage its effects and, in passing, to draw profits from it. In Chapter 2 we focus on one of the most important of these 'antibodies' – one that also has a long history, but whose importance is constantly growing as the ecological crisis deepens. That is, insurance for climatic risks, one of the forms that environmental finance today assumes.

2
Financializing Nature: Insuring Climatic Risks

Nature stops breathing in the body of commodities.
Alfred Sohn-Rethel

In 1781 the *Zong*, a slave ship chartered by a Liverpool-based merchant company, threw 133 slaves overboard close to Jamaica.[1] The captain justified his action: given the mishaps that the ship had run into since departing from São Tomé, off the west coast of Africa, the journey had taken longer than expected, food and water had started running out and there was the risk of disease overwhelming the crew. In order to save it, he had to get rid of some of the slaves. Not long afterward, the shipowners in England demanded that their insurer compensate them for the slaves that they had lost. As always in this kind of case, they had taken out an insurance policy covering all the boat's cargo. During the court case held in London in 1783, the massacre was treated not as a murder – the murder of the 133 slaves – but as an insurance litigation over how well founded the compensation claim was. In legal terms, after all, the slaves were reduced to a 'cargo'. The shipowners lost their case against the insurer, on the basis that a reasonable quantity of food and water was still available on the boat at the moment that these events played out and that the ship's delay, which was due to the captain's errors, could have been avoided. He had calculated that the insurance payment would be superior to what he would have obtained by selling the slaves upon his arrival in the Americas. This massacre stirred the emotions of numerous contemporaries and was one of the founding acts in the movement for the abolition of slavery.

The *Zong* episode demonstrates that colonization and slavery have always been linked to the insurance sector. At that time, imperial adventure was too risky for investors to throw themselves into without any safety net. British imperialism – and, before it, the Genoese and Dutch cycles of accumulation – was an ocean imperialism.[2] Right from its origins, it met obstacles along the way and was particularly subject to climatic hazards. For this reason, if capital were to expand globally, there had to be some mechanism established in order to protect investment.[3] This mechanism was none other than insurance (and finance more generally), which provided security for commodities and made it possible for something of their capitalist value to survive, even when they were destroyed in shipwrecks, fires, epidemics, pillage and so on, since the investor could still pocket his indemnity.

In this sense, it is hardly astonishing that modern insurance took off in the seventeenth century in the domain of maritime insurance. As well as an exchange-value and a use-value, commodities have an 'insurance-value'. Insured commodities generate value, since the moment of their possible destruction is anticipated in advance.[4] In the *Zong* case, the extraction of 'insurance-value' related to human beings becoming transformed into slaves – that is, into commodities – but capitalism could also subject anything to such a process.

Insurance for natural risks dates back to the threshold of the modern age and even, without doubt, to Antiquity. In the sixteenth century, when the discovery of the Americas and the improvement of navigation techniques propelled Europe across the oceans, vessels and their cargoes were insured against the possibility of shipwreck.[5] What was then called *respondentia* allowed shipowners to avoid being bankrupted by losing a ship. The principle was a simple one: the lender provided a certain amount to the shipowner, of the order of the price of the cargo. If the cargo arrived at its proper destination this latter would hand back the lender's money, with interest. In the event of shipwreck, he would keep it. The seas were still far from secure at the time, to the extent of posing a constant risk to the international circulation of commodities. The exponential increase in the flows of goods and people across the following centuries, with the expansion of capitalism, gave rise to a growing sophistication in insurance techniques.[6] The emergence of a world market, the imperialism to which it gave rise and insurance against natural risks (and other types of risks) were, in this sense, inextricably linked. Yet it is rare that theorists of imperialism mention the insurance dimension of this phenomenon.

Triangular trade was, indeed, one of the main activities whose premiums fed the insurance sector that emerged in the seventeenth century. The surge in insurance premiums, linked to the massive rise in slave transportation and, more generally, in worldwide sea trade, allowed this sector to develop. In this sense, modern insurance originally began in connection with slavery. But there is more. The global expansion of capitalism in this epoch was conditional upon the emergence of finance. This is what has been called the 'financial revolution' of the late seventeenth and early eighteenth centuries.[7] Finance made it possible, among other things, to ancipate future profits – that is, to use still-non-existent funds for investment.

Then again, finance itself could not have developed without insurance – not only because insurance allowed it to cover financial risk (in the event that the promise of future profits was not realized) but also because it constituted a field of investment that was in itself profitable and towards which capitals flowed.[8] If triangular trade allowed the development of insurance and if insurance allowed the development of finance, it is clear that financialization and slavery were far from alien to one another. The fact that Atlantic trade became so massive in extent, compared to other regions, is in part explained by its interconnection with finance and insurance.

Insuring natural risks does not regard the maritime sector alone. Ever since the threshold of the modern age, other types of (natural and/or social) disasters that also pose a risk to capital accumulation have been the object of insurance, from hurricanes to earthquakes, floods, droughts, fires and pandemics like influenza. As the economy grew in the wake of the industrial revolution, the value of what was susceptible to loss (and thus insurance) continually increased. People also became the object of insurance with the appearance of 'life insurance', guaranteeing that a certain sum would be paid out in the event of the insured person's death, or if they lived beyond a certain date. Life insurance is a form of insuring nature, since in the last instance what is being insured is bodies – life. Thus a *Compagnie royale d'assurance vie* [Royal Life Insurance Company] was created in France at the end of the eighteenth century. It was banned after the French Revolution, on the grounds that it distorted individual autonomy and responsibility, and was later recreated in different form at the beginning of the nineteenth century.[9] Life insurance was the object of a great number of protests in the nineteenth and twentieth centuries, in that it gave the impression of quantifying life, thus contravening still-deeply-anchored moral and religious principles.[10] Since then, however, capitalist commodification has done its work.

Financial markets 'plugged into' nature[11]

Although insurance for natural disasters has a very long history, it is currently a rapidly expanding market. One section of this market has seen particularly striking success in recent years, namely financial bonds that transfer climatic risks, for example weather derivatives and catastrophe bonds, or cat bonds. These securities speak to the growing interconnection of finance with nature over the last two to three decades. They belong to the sector of finance now included under the name 'environmental finance'. They entrust insurance for financial risks and everything that goes with it – insurance premiums, risk evaluation, compensating victims . . . – to the finance markets. Whereas previously the insurance market rested on three components – namely insurers, reinsurers and the state as the organizer of the market's legal framework and insurer of last resort – a fourth actor has now been added to the list: finance.

This growth in the power of environmental finance results from the interweaving of two crises, as well as the increased inequalities to which they give rise. First, an economic crisis. In the first half of the 1970s, capitalism entered into a deep crisis, at the moment when the long growth period of the *Trente Glorieuses* was interrupted. This 'long return', as Robert Brenner put it, set the profit rate in crisis and it has continued to be depressed ever since.[12] It has also increased inequalities, both within and among states. The crisis that began in 2007–8, in which we find ourselves still today, is but the most recent manifestation of this long-term crisis.

How has capital reacted to this fall in profitability? In two ways: on the one hand, privatizing everything that had previously escaped market control, meaning public services but also biodiversity, knowledges, the human genome . . . and here, privatization means subjecting these things to the logic of profit in order to try to drive profitability upward. On the other hand, through financialization; that is to say, investing not in the so-called 'real' or 'productive' economy – that is, precisely the economy where the profit rate is declining – but instead in finance, which allows the realization of major (fictitious) profits, up till the moment when crisis arrives.

Insurance in general and insurance for natural disasters in particular has been captured by capital's dual movement of privatization and financialization. There is a neoliberal regime in insurance, just as in other domains: pensions, scientific research, enterprise management or global trade. Yet it is rare that histories of neoliberalism take into account the insurance-specific dimension of this phenomenon. Insurance is a crucial sector of social life. It reflects the prevalent conception of solidarity – the 'social bond', as we so trivially put it nowadays.

To take out insurance is to transfer to others some or all of the risks inherent in the human condition and, more particularly, to industrial civilization. The manner in which this other is 'constructed' is thus a political concern *par excellence*. Insurance is also an index representative of the time that a society creates for itself, or more precisely, the concurrent conceptions of time that we find therein, since by definition insurance concerns a future risk.

Taking the insurance regime prevalent within a given social world, we can say the same thing that Fredric Jameson says about utopia; it always entails an implicit theory of the future, which expresses the way in which a collective projects itself into the future.[13]

The other crisis that explains the growing strength of environmental finance is, of course, the ecological crisis. This exacerbates capitalism's instability and as a consequence calls for the investment-protection mechanism of insurance – and finance more generally – to be strengthened. These are the 'antibodies' secreted by the system, to which we referred at the end of the previous chapter. Given the multiplication and aggravation of natural disasters, the ecological crisis also induces a rise in the global cost of insurance. It thus exerts a downward pressure on the profit rate. This leads insurance and reinsurance companies to introduce new insurance techniques and new means of spreading risks. First among these is the securitization of climatic risks, which, in turn, provides capitalism with fresh opportunities to rake in profits.

On account of these crises, nature is thus ever more subjected to finance – indeed, subsumed to it, in the sense that Marx spoke of 'real subsumption'. Writing the political history of nature and understanding why it is a battlefield, demands that we grasp the multiple and contradictory processes of which it is the product. This chapter's objective is to break through the veil of mystery hanging over this financialization of nature.

Principles of insurance

If we are to understand what is currently happening with regard to climatic risks, then we must indispensably interrogate the means of insurance's functioning. The financialization of insurance has resulted from the appearance of 'new risks' over the last century, including environmental changes. That is not to say that such risks were absent from the history of capitalism up till that point – far from it. But our own epoch is unprecedented in terms of both the intensification and the concomitance of these new risks. They have set traditional insurance in crisis, giving rise to the appearance of original insurance techniques.

What is an insurance? The principle of this mechanism is a simple one: an entity A, for example a person, hands a premium to an entity B on a regular basis, most often an insurance company, which commits to indemnify A in the event of an accident, according to the terms of a pre-established contract. The contract specifies the amount that A pays to B, the indemnity due from B to A in the event of an accident and also determines what counts as an appropriate claim. As we know, when this does occur there can be debate over this point, since it is in the insurer's interest to restrict as much as possible the scope within which indemnities apply. The level of the premium is, in principle, proportional to the risk of accidents occurring: the higher the risk, the higher the premium. It is also subject to the insured party's reputation, for example in the case of a motorist who has behaved imprudently in the past, from which his future behaviour is extrapolated.

In practice, the rate of the premium is set in correspondence with some certainly rather less 'pure' mechanisms: the construction of monopolies, state subsidies, the exclusion of certain categories of insured party, etc. The risk is transferred in space, in the sense that it is extended to individuals other than the person or organization running that risk and also in time, in that the payment of the premium begins before any harm is done and possibly even without any claim ever occurring.

This seemingly simple definition relies on two principles.[14] The first is the mutualization of risk. The number of insurance policies that the insurer contracts must be sufficiently great than the premiums it takes in are superior to the amount of indemnities that it has to pay out to the insured in the event of an accident. In other words, reimbursing these costs must not lead it to insolvency, and this demands that it must hold sufficient liquidity at any given moment. It is also necessary that the risks insured are weakly correlated, or, to put that another way, that each of these claims occur statistically independently of the others. Thus motor insurance is possible only because not every motorist will suffer a car accident all at once. In short, some people's premiums serve to indemnify other people's damages. A major part of insurers' energies is devoted to implementing strategies of risk diversification. In order to keep an eye on the indemnities that they will have to pay out over the course of a year, insurers take recourse to the law of large numbers. Applied to insurance, this means 'the greater the number of contracts are combined, the more it allows – all other things being equal – an (average) fore-sight' of the payouts.[15] Though it is not possible to foresee if and when such and such motorist will be involved in an accident, the number of traffic accidents – and thus the amount of indemnities to be paid out – varies little year by year, making it possible to make forecasts based on this figure.

As we shall see, one of the specificities of the 'new risks', which include climate change, is that this clause about the non-correlation of risks no longer applies. A terrorist attack or a hurricane affects an entire geographical area at the same moment, facing insurers with the obligation to indemnify a large number of insured parties simultaneously. This means that it is frequently the case that these 'new risks' lead to the bankruptcy of certain insurers. Nine Florida insurers were bankrupted after Hurricane Andrew in 1992, one of the first cases where the costs surpassed one billion dollars.[16] This is the reason why the possibility of insuring such risks poses unprecedented problems.

A second principle of insurance is the 'inversion of the production cycle'. This principle stipulates that the insured party pays the premium before any accident occurs, without knowing if it will occur, when it will occur and how much the losses will amount to. Naturally, it is ruled out on prin-ciple that anyone could insure for damage that has already been done, or an event whose occurrence can be predicted with certainty. As such, it is decisively important that the object of the insurance be uncertain in character. This is sometimes threatened by what insurers call a 'moral hazard'. This expression designates those cases where there is an asymmetry of information between the insurer and the insured party. Here, the insured party is capable of exercising some influence on the damage done, for example through careless driving or neglecting to protect his home from flood risk. As such, he will have more complete information than the insurer does as to the probability that an accident will happen, or how significant the damage will be if it does. Insurers, for their part, do what they can to gather the most detailed possible information on the situation that is being insured for. An insurer only insures what it is able to calculate and classify and for this reason it needs the maximum possible information. Insurance companies also have an interest in forcing insured parties to take the necessary preventative measures in order to keep the risk under control and in refusing to insure them if they do not consent to this. Beyond diversifying risks, preventing them outright makes up an important part of insurers' activity.

Information is thus a question of decisive importance in any insurance procedure. This has led theorists of insurance to draw a distinction between *risk* and *uncertainty*. The first to do so was the economist Frank Knight, who advanced this distinction in his 1921 work *Risk, Uncertainty and Profit*.[17] Knight was one of the founders of the Chicago School of Economics, the school of Milton Friedman and Gary Becker, and was also a member of the Mont-Pèlerin Society. His neoliberal pedigree is, therefore, impeccable. Risk is an uncertainty whose probability can be judged, and thus it can be insured. Transforming uncertainty into risk supposes having available as complete a set of information as possible. Information also makes it possible to 'price' risk, as insurers put it, determining the amount of the premiums and indemnities involved. It is sometimes the case that the impossibility of judging the probability of an uncertainty – that is, the impossibility of transforming it into a risk – leads insurers to pull out of a given market. This could be the case if disasters owing to environmental change led to growing costs that became difficult to predict. In general, however, insurers do prove capable of implementing the strategies necessary to constructing profitable markets.

Modern insurance is inextricably bound up with reinsurance, which follows it as its shadow. Reinsurance is 'the insurers' insurance',[18] according to an expression commonplace in this field. For the insurers, it consists of protecting themselves against what they consider to be major risks, by taking out insurance on the insurance policies themselves. The same mechanism operates here as at the level below: the insurer pays a premium to the reinsurer, who will pay it indemnities in the event that an accident occurs. The reinsurer will most often reinvest these premiums in finance, with the profits from this serving to pay for its reimbursement of the insurers. That is the reason why, since the nineteenth century, reinsurers have been among the protagonists of international finance. There are numerous types of reinsurance contracts.[19] One type stipulates, for example, that the reinsurer take charge of all the indemnification costs for a claim that exceed a certain amount, while the insurer will be responsible for everything beneath that level.

The biggest reinsurers in the world today are Munich Re, founded in 1880 and Swiss Re, founded in 1863. Historically, the oldest reinsurance company is Cologne Re, founded in 1846, which, after its fusion with various other companies, is now called Gen (General) Re. Reinsurers first arrived on the scene following the fires that ravaged the great modern cities in the nineteenth century. In 1842 a fire that broke out in Hamburg bankrupted several German insurers, giving rise to the emergence of this sector. The founding period of modern reinsurance corresponds precisely to the era of the industrial revolution. Because of industrialization, it was in this period that the amounts of insured assets that insurers had to deal with became exorbitant and impossible to take on without outside support. The insurance and reinsurance market has grown relentlessly ever since then. After the Second World War it grew twice as quickly as the developed countries' GDP. The unprecedented development of advanced capitalist societies during the *Trente Glorieuses* was not, it should go without saying, extraneous to this tendency.

Reinsurance supposes a higher degree of mutualization of risks than does insurance. This 'mutualization-squared', so to speak, makes it possible to push down the overall cost of insurance, since when insurers reinsure – thus protecting themselves against the risks of particularly high losses – they are able to reduce the premium levels they demand of those who take out policies with them. The volumes of finance handled by the reinsurance industry are higher than those for insurance, since they come from the pooled premiums of numerous insurers. That is the reason why reinsurance often concerns the most costly risks, such as terrorism, natural disasters, accidents involving technology . . . or the ones that are most correlated among themselves. However, since reinsurers first appeared they have operated on a global scale. As such, they count among the earliest globalized companies. Their capacity to deal with particularly high indemnities is the fruit of a strategy of diversifying contracts across geographical areas and economic sectors. Once again, the principle of seeking to aggregate risks that have a weak correlation among themselves applies here. Indeed, it is less likely that multiple geographical areas will simultaneously be affected by a natural or technological disaster, or that crisis will simultaneously strike multiple different branches of the economy.

New risks?

This modern insurance mechanism was hit hard by the emergence of 'new risks', starting in the second half of the twentieth century. When it comes to history, claims of novelty should always be treated with some caution: more often than not, the novelty concerned results from intensification, hybridization and the making-visible of processes that were already previously at work, rather than radical innovations.[20] Be that as it may, these new risks do in part escape the reach of the insurance mechanism that we have described, either because the indemnity levels that they imply are too high, including for reinsurers, or because the nature of these risks makes them hard to insure, since the principles of insurance, such as we have presented them, are difficult to apply to these cases. This leads to the emergence of a new insurance regime – one in which finance occupies a central position.

The notion of 'catastrophe' is a relative one – that is to say, it is historically and geographically variable.[21] In the Judeo-Christian world it has an evident religious connotation. The literature on insurance frequently cites a distinction between 'catastrophes' and 'cataclysms', as proposed by David Cutler and Richard Zeckhauser.[22] A catastrophic event is one where the damages amount to more than $25 million; above $5 billion and it is cataclysmic. This seemingly abstract distinction is explained by the wish to make calculations and thus to classify events in advance. Such a distinction dates back to 1997. Since then, the upward shift in the costs of claims has made it necessary to update these figures.

A number of different types of risk are ravaging the insurance sector, from terrorism to technological risks and the multiplication of natural disasters – including because of climate change. How so? Firstly, as we have said, because the financial cost of the catastrophes that these risks induce is very high and constantly increasing. The reinsurer Swiss Re produces very complete annual data on the extent of these catastrophes' human and material cost, collated in a journal entitled *Sigma*.[23] It is interesting to note, in passing, that states are not today the only producers of data of this type and that private actors like insurers have sufficient human and material resources as to allow them to compete with state statistics agencies. The data produced by Swiss Re principally concern insured assets, or, to put that another way, the sums that insurers and reinsurers have paid out to their clients and not assets in general. This tends to distort the scale of the catastrophes concerned, since the level of insured assets, relative to the overall assets destroyed, varies from one society to another. For example, the insurance sector is much less developed in Burkina Faso than in France, since taking out insurance requires that you have the means necessary to do so. As such, it is estimated that only 3 per cent of the assets lost in catastrophes in developing countries are insured. This figure rises to more than 40 per cent for developed countries.[24] This leads the available data to provide a systematic underestimation of the losses suffered in developing countries.

The costliest catastrophe in history in terms of insured damages – since records began in 1970 – was Hurricane Katrina, which struck the New Orleans region in 2005. Five years after this catastrophe occurred, its material cost was estimated at $75bn (adjusted for inflation) and $150bn also including the estimated damage to non-insured assets. Katrina ranks as the costliest on account of the devastating power of the hurricane, as well as the mistakes and unpreparedness of the US authorities in handling the situation. But this also results from the fact that it struck the richest country in the world, for which reason a higher proportion of material assets were insured.

Listed next in the ranking of the costliest catastrophes in history are the 2011 earthquake – followed by a tsunami – in Japan (coming in at $35bn), which also gave rise to the Fukushima nuclear catastrophe; 1992's Hurricane Andrew ($25bn) in the United States; and the 11 September 2001 terrorist attacks ($24bn), with this latter being the costliest of the events that Swiss Re classifies as a 'technical' catastrophe, meaning an event unrelated to natural phenomena. In France in 2003, year of the heatwave, the aggregated cost of natural disasters rose to more than €2bn, a record figure. Over the last twenty years the main natural risk has been flooding, followed by drought. //

Naturally, such figures ought to be treated with some caution, particularly insofar as catastrophes are liable to generate effects staggered over time and which are thus difficult to evaluate.

Thus, a hurricane in Taiwan may not only destroy material assets and claim human victims, but also interrupt global circuits of production or assembly, for example in the field of IT, in which Taiwan is an important link in the chain. It could also slow naval transit in the Formosa Straits (which separate the island from continental China), which massive commercial flows pass through. Given the acceleration of globalization since the 1970s, 'global commodity chains' have tended to become increasingly longer, extending across the globe.[25] A production accident (whether natural or technical in character) taking place at a certain point will compromise the whole chain in a more or less lasting way, generating significant insurance costs. To take one further example, when response workers contracted lung conditions during their intervention at the Twin Towers site on 11 September 2001, due to their prolonged contact with dust and rubble, this took some time to manifest itself; often even several years. Its bearing on the (public and private) insurance system was thus spread out over time.

A disaster may have a very high material cost yet not much human cost – or vice versa. The deadliest catastrophes since 1970, in terms of the number of human victims, were the storms and flooding resulting from the Bhola cyclone in Bangladesh (at that time, East Pakistan) and the Indian state of Bengal in 1970, which claimed around 300,000 victims. In third place we find the 2010 earthquake in Haiti, with 222,000 victims. The 2003 heatwave and drought in Europe, which led to 35,000 deaths, is twelfth on the list; moreover, this is the highest-ranked of the listed catastrophes that were located in Europe, whereas Europe and the United States dominate the top ranks of the table classifying the financial cost of catastrophes. This demonstrates – if further proof were needed – the impact that economic development has on the mortality rates resulting from such events. Lower down in the classification, we find the 1984 accident at the Union Carbide chemicals plant – a US multinational factory in Bhopal, India – which claimed 6,000 lives.

Swiss Re accounts for a total of 325 catastrophes for 2011 – the most recent year for which figures are available – 175 of which were 'natural' and 150 'technical'. It is interesting to note that the reinsurer counts the 2011 'Arab Spring' as a 'technical catastrophe'. The material losses suffered in this revolutionary process were significant ones and in Egypt 846 people lost their lives. In the last instance, for an insurer any event that surpasses a certain amount of indemnity pay-outs to the insured counts as a catastrophe; it is a purely quantitative definition of catastrophe. Nonetheless, in principle insurers' accounting for catastrophes excludes everything belonging to the order of wars, revolutions, crimes against humanity and other 'states of exception'.

The Japanese earthquake was the highest-ranking disaster of 2011. New Zealand also suffered an earthquake, and the hurricane season in the United States was particularly virulent, even if none of them was as devastating as Hurricane Katrina or Andrew. There was also deadly flooding in Thailand from July onward. In 2011, for the second consecutive year, technical catastrophes seem to have been less numerous than natural ones. According to Swiss Re, the number of technical ones has continued to decline since 2005, whereas since 1970 natural disasters have continued their historical tendency to increase. We should not draw any hasty conclusions as to this apparent fall in technical catastrophes. This tendency may be the fruit of chance or of improved safety measures, but it could equally be the result of the restriction of insurers' reimbursement conditions since, as we have seen, they mainly account for the catastrophes that gave rise to pay-outs. However, there is good reason to bet that even if climate change is not not the only cause of the rise of natural disasters – and in this field, it is difficult to establish causality – it is evidently one of the contributing factors.

As capitalism develops, urbanization and demographic growth relentlessly continue to increase.[26] For example, the population of California has tripled since 1950, which makes earthquakes and landslides in this state all the more deadly. California, Florida and Japan are three regions that frequently fall victim to natural disasters, with their population density, as well as building density, having grown across the whole twentieth century. In many locations, urbanization and demographic growth have proceeded without regard for the environment, and this has aggravated the potentially deadly character of such disasters. In this sense, the humid areas of Louisiana have been the object of uncontrolled urban development over recent decades. These wetlands had previously represented a buffer zone, protecting the land and the inhabitants from hurricanes. The effect of development in making this environment more fragile is a significant factor in explaining the level of damage that Hurricane Katrina caused in this state in 2005. So the rising cost of insuring climatic risks is closely linked to demographic, urban and economic development.

The growth in life expectancy is a corollary of this tendency, whose environmental impact is obvious. In Florida, for example, ever greater numbers of pensioners are making their homes on the coast, which drives up the rate of urbanization.[27] These coasts often fall victim to hurricanes and other natural disasters; 80 per cent of insured assets in Florida are situated close to the coast, in regions that are thus subject to this risk.[28] In the United States more generally, the value of insured assets in coastal areas rose by 70 per cent in the 1990s, reaching more than $3tn by the end of the decade. Certain parts of southern France find themselves in a similar situation. Between 1988 and 2007, the *départements* of Aude, Hérault and Le Gard were the most affected by flooding.[29] A causal chain thus links rising life expectancy, urbanization and the insurance costs resulting from these two tendencies.

This process should be understood in relation to a general tendency for 'production costs' to increase as capitalism develops. As Immanuel Wallerstein has shown, three long-term movements explain the rise in production costs across the course of history.[30] First of all there was the rural exodus, which meant the transformation of huge numbers of peasants into wage-workers. While a large proportion of them could, until that point, have counted (at least in part) on feeding themselves through agriculture, their arrival in the cities now left them entirely dependent on the wages paid to them by their employers, thus both increasing the share of surplus-value transformed into wages and, proportionally, diminishing profits. This was followed by an exponentially increasing demand to pay for these populations' wellbeing – in health, education, pensions – particularly during the *Trente Glorieuses*; and this, too, immobilized major capital volumes. This is one aspect of the 'state financial crisis', a theme to which we will return shortly.

A third factor in increasing production costs is the exhaustion of nature. For many centuries, nature has provided capitalism with cheap raw materials and other natural resources.[31] Previously, it also largely managed to absorb the waste products of capitalist production. Yet it is today more and more difficult for nature to fulfil these two functions – as both input and output – meaning that these functions themselves become more and more expensive. The rising cost of capitalism's relation with nature pushes down profit rates.

The ontology of catastrophe

These new risks are characterized by the phenomenon of 'hypercorrelation'. As we have said, the risks that an insurer takes on must be sufficiently uncorrelated that it does not have to pay out to too many insured parties all at once. With these new risks, this principle of non-correlation enters into crisis. The catastrophes we mentioned above affected hundreds of thousands or even millions of people and, at the same time, colossal volumes of material assets. To put that another way, they strike entire regions, which forces insurers to deal with costs that are often beyond their capabilities and sometimes to pull back from the market. That is what happened in the United States following the 11 September 2001 attacks, when insurers' contracts dropped terrorism coverage, before the state forcibly pushed them back onto this market (their retreat from it in fact having been a means of compelling the state to take on an ever greater share of insuring for such attacks: a privatization of profits and socialization of losses – for that is how capitalism works).[32] These catastrophes affect many lines of insurance simultaneously: life insurance, disability annuities, the interruption of economic activities and damages for both assets and people.[33] Moreover, they are liable to disrupting an area in a lasting manner, which can also have major economic consequences. This itself drives the evolution of the insurance sector. As we saw with the creation of reinsurance following the city fires of the nineteenth century, it is often the case that innovations in this sector follow on from disasters.

A catastrophe is ontologically different from more ordinary hazards like car accidents. When there is a car accident, even a serious one, a restricted number of people will be affected. Moreover, as we have said, if a single accident is, by definition, unpredictable, the combined amount of accidents in a given time period responds to the law of large numbers. Conversely, a catastrophe affects everyone in a given area. For a longer or shorter period, it will interrupt the normal course of social life – which is obviously not true in the case of a car accident. The law of large numbers does not apply here; this is, instead, a one-off event. This means that it is difficult for insurers to anticipate their losses in advance and, therefore, to implement diversification strategies appropriate to the relevant risks. In insurers' jargon, rare events are called 'tails' of loss distribution, which are unlikely to occur. *Tail risk* is an expression employed in the financial world in general to designate extreme risks liable, for example, to lead to the loss of an entire financial portfolio.

It is harder to determine the new risks' probability than was the case with traditional risks. The difficulty in putting together trustworthy data on these risks means that insurers do not always manage to put a price on this uncertainty and they are thus unable to set premium levels. A further consequence of hypercorrelation is that it blurs the distinction between private and public.[34] A car accident is a private hazard, even if a major accident can also cause a temporary problem of public concern, or even be important enough to stir public opinion. A catastrophe of a type with 11 September 2001, or the 2004 tsunami in the Indian Ocean off the coast of Java – with its 210,000 deaths – is a public phenomenon, precisely because it affects an entire geographical area. The proliferation of this kind of catastrophe in recent decades and, particularly, the multiplication of natural disasters due to climate change, thus sets in crisis the distinction between public and private, one of the foundations of the modern social world. It also changes the state's role in handling these catastrophes.

Risk and postmodernity

This ontology of the new risks has given rise to one of the most influential of contemporary social theories: Ulrich Beck's 'risk society', was formulated in his book of the same name published in 1986.[35] The British sociologist Anthony Giddens, well known as the main theorist of Tony Blair's 'Third Way', is also a partisan of this approach.[36] Beck's name came to prominence in the debates on 'postmodernity' that raged across the 1980s and 1990s. At issue, here, was whether we had left behind modernity and its values – science, reason, progress, justice, inequality' – such as to enter into 'postmodernity', or if, conversely, these values were still the active forces in societal organization. From Jean-François Lyotard to Jürgen Habermas via Fredric Jameson, David Harvey and Perry Anderson, contemporary thinkers gave widely varied responses to this question.

Beck's highly original answer rested on insurance. In his eyes, the decisive criterion for explaining the passage from modernity to postmodernity – which he calls a 'second' or 'reflexive' modernity – is insurability. With postmodernity, certain risks have become so costly that they are no longer insurable according to the criteria of modern insurance. They escape human control, even if it is humans that create them, both because they are unpredictable and because their consequences are socially unmanageable. Insofar as modernity largely rested on the gradual mastering of risks and, more generally, on man's subjection of nature, uninsurability symptomizes our exit from modernity.

Beck devotes particular attention to technological risks; for example the 1986 Chernobyl nuclear disaster. Such risks do not respect borders, be they spatial (the cloud let out by

Chernobyl did not stop at national boundaries), social (it affected rich and poor without distinction between classes) or temporal ones (its consequences will become apparent across many decades or even centuries). They prefigure the end of the nation-state, which is defined by the fact that it is territorially delimited and therefore incapable of handling such risks. These risks thus call for the emergence of a new 'cosmopolitism' – a vision of which Beck has become the champion in recent years.[37]

For Beck, uninsurability is thus the foundation of the post-modern condition. However, this conclusion ought to be seriously qualified. What Beck does not see is, that while traditional insurers and reinsurers are not capable of insuring nuclear risks by themselves, since the 1960s (that is, since the appearance of the civil nuclear industry) they have given rise to insurance 'pools', in which the state and sometimes even several states are stakeholders.[38] In France this pool is called 'Assuratome',[39] and its vocation is to provide coverage for the civil nuclear industry. The recent Fukushima disaster set multiple insurance procedures into effect. One year later, it was estimated that it had cost each of Munich Re and AIG €3bn and Partner Re something of the order of €600m. It thus demonstrated that insurance has not ceased functioning in the contemporary world – including for risks that relate to the most costly and sophisticated of technologies.[40] More-over, the financialization of insurance – a phenomenon that Beck does not take into consideration – is concomitant with the emergence of new risks, transforming insurability as a problematic. We will return to this point in a moment.

François Ewald is a theorist of 'risk', close to Beck. A former member of the *Gauche Prolétarienne*, one of the branches of 1970s French Maoism, and an assistant of Michel Foucault's at the Collège de France, Ewald then became a 'thinking head' for the *Fédération française des sociétés d'assurance* (FFSA) and the MEDEF,[41] and today he is direc-tor of the *École nationale d'assurances*.[42] He devoted his doctoral thesis to the history of the welfare state, under Fou-cault's supervision. He was particularly interested in the evo-lution of the juridical treatment of occupational risks. At the end of the nineteenth century the idea emerged that accidents and other hazards of the workplace should not be imputed to individuals, but were instead a risk inherent to industrial activity. In Ewald's view this break with the idea of 'responsibility' (and first of all, the bosses' responsibility) – as well as its replacement with the idea of 'risk' – marked the true beginning of the modern era. Unlike responsibility, risk is not the product of any intentionality – it is an impersonal principle. Ewald then concerned himself with other types of risk, including technological risk. In the pages of *Le Débat* magazine he also theorized, together with Denis Kessler (at that time, FFSA president and MEDEF vice-president), 'the marriage of risk and politics'.[43] They, together with others, formulated a distinction between 'riskophile' and 'riskophobe' individuals, declaring that man is not a political or social animal – contrary to what Aristotle thought – but an animal naturally predisposed to taking risks. This was the era in which the MEDEF launched its vision of a 're-foundation of society', with the ambition of breaking with the programme of the *Conseil national de la Résistance*.[44] In France as elsewhere, the ideology of 'risk' and 'empowerment' is a stakeholder in the emergence of neoliberalism.

Adventures in insurability

The insurance sector has undergone profound changes over recent decades. For example, we have seen the emergence of the new category of so-called 'development' risks, a variant of technological risk.[45] These risks express an essential dimension of all technical innovation: namely that, even long after a product first comes to market, it can prove to have damaging consequences for public health, unforeseen by its producers. The utmost example of this phenomenon is asbestos, which, though it is not a catastrophe properly speaking – that is, a one-off event interrupting the course of normal social life – to this day remains the phenomenon that has inflicted the greatest costs on the US insurance industry.[46] (The first studies to establish the harmful character of asbestos did not suffice to prevent workers from continuing to be exposed to it for many years, adding a dimension of criminality, pure and simple, to this development risk.) Development risk can result from a problem in a product's design – such as in a car model, as exemplified by the 2010 recall of the Mercedes A-Class on account of a defect in its petrol tank – or from some sort of external interference (whether deliberate or otherwise) in the fabrication process, such as when traces of benzene were discovered in a dozen bottles of Perrier in the United States in the early 1990s, leading the company to pull hundreds of millions of bottles off the market.

Development risks have considerable consequences for the insurance industry. So-called 'commercial liability insurance' – including the particular case of recall insurances, which cover a manufacturer's product recalls – has experienced significant growth over recent decades, of the order of 10 per cent a year.[47] The benzene affair is said to have cost Perrier more than a billion dollars. Of course, these development risks are nothing new. Ever since the beginning of the industrial era, certain products have proven harmful upon use, either harming their producers or consumers directly or polluting the environment and thus affecting these latter indirectly.[48] What has changed is public opinion's sensitivity to such situations, as a result of our increased knowledge of these risks and their health consequences. As Jürgen Habermas explains, we are seeing a process in which science is 'visibilizing' new hazards, allowing us to perceive risks that we could not have noticed previously – in other words, risks that had been 'silent killers'.[49] The 'judicialization' of social relations – meaning, the increasing importance of the law in regulating disputes – is a further element of this question. The development of scientific knowledge, of law and of insurance are, in this sense, closely linked.

Terrorism has also had an important impact on the insurance sector. As we have noted, 11 September 2001 was one of the costliest events in the history of insurance. Of course, the fact that the city struck by the attacks was New York, one of the world's richest cities and a global financial centre, is by no means unrelated to these particularly high costs. London is another global city affected by terrorism. The Irish Republican Army (IRA) struck the UK capital on numerous occasions, including the City itself in April 1993. The cost of the attack was estimated at one billion pounds sterling. These events gave rise to a far-reaching restructuring of the insurance sector.[50] First of all, the massive losses that the insurers incurred due to these attacks led them to limit their exposure to terrorism; that is to say, they now excluded coverage for terrorist attacks from their insurance contracts. The British state forced them to go back on this decision and instead established an insurance pool under its own aegis called Pool Re, bringing together some two hundred insurers.[51] Pool Re functions like a reinsurance company and it is itself reinsured by the state above certain levels of losses.

Today financial risks are also massively insured. The interconnection of finance and insurance, which emerged at the moment of the 'financial revolution' of the seventeenth century, has in fact continued to deepen ever further. Among other things, financial insurance concerns the risks of exchange and of credit. Indeed, the evolution of the exchange rates between two different currencies is liable to produce considerable variations in a multinational's profits, given that its centres of production and sales will be scattered across all four corners of the globe. For this reason, today there are a whole range of insurance mechanisms for dealing with this problem. Derivatives products – to which we will return – count among the most important of these mechanisms.

One of the acronyms that became widely used in media during the crisis that began in 2008 was 'CDS', meaning 'Credit Default Swap'. These financial products allow an investor to cover a position that is at risk from the possible failure of a third party, for example a state that declares a payments default.[52] The swap is a sort of insurance, derived from another bond – for example, a sovereign debt – which is termed 'underlying'. The seller, in this swap, is the insurer and the buyer is the insured party. The latter pays a premium to the former, as in a traditional insurance policy. If there is a 'credit event', declared as such by the competent financial authorities, then an indemnity is paid out to the insured party. Swaps were created by the investment bank JP Morgan, in the United States. The total sum of contracted swaps in that country alone is estimated at between 45 and 60 billion dollars. The structure of this market is so complex that no one is able to predict what would be the consequences of a massive CDS trigger following a credit event. That is the reason why at the moment of Greece's latent default in

Summer 2011, the European authorities took great care to avoid its bankruptcy overtly being identified as such.

Cat (catastrophe) bonds

Among the 25 costliest natural disasters of the 1970–2010 period, more than half occurred after 2001. The number of category four or five hurricanes has doubled in 35 years, with five representing the maximum wind strength. And among the ten costliest natural disasters of the last fifty years, six took place in 2004 and 2005. The cost of these natural disasters is ever more exorbitant for the insurance industry, even without counting the fact that as we have seen it is simultaneously having to face up to other risks. All this has led this industry to add an extra level to the existing insurance mechanism, as we have already described, and turn to the financial markets in order to increase both its potential indemnification and its profits. This phenomenon is called the securitization (a 'security' in the sense of the financial asset) of climatic risks. It makes up part of the general phenomenon of the financialization of nature, such as we have seen over the last several decades. As we said at the start of this chapter, financialization is a phenomenon typical of the neoliberal age, which has seen numerous sectors that previously evaded market control now being captured by its logic. And nature is one of these sectors.

One of the most fascinating financial products generated by the securitization of natural risks takes the name 'cat bond'. A bond is a loan title or fraction of debt that can be exchanged on a financial market and which is 'quoted' (it has a price, which fluctuates). A bond can be public – and is, then, a treasury bond – or it can be issued by a private organization.

Cat bonds are fractions of debt and their particularity is that they are based not on the debt that a state incurs in order to renew its infrastructure, or that an enterprise incurs in order to finance innovation, but on nature and natural disasters.

In short, their 'underlying' is nature. They concern a natural disaster that has not yet occurred, that, while possible, may well not occur and that we know will bring major human and material damage. The object of cat bonds is to spread natural risks as widely as possible in space and time, so as to diminish their financial effect. Since financial markets are today extended across a world scale, securitization spreads out these risks to a maximum extent.

Cat bonds do not only concern natural disasters. Over recent years, insurers and reinsurers have protected themselves against all types of excess mortality (or 'extreme mortality', to use the jargon currently in vogue in this sector), of whatever cause. The recent flu pandemics, swine flu in 2009 and bird flu since 2003, have thus led to the issuing of cat bonds covering the insurers in case of a mass death toll.[53] Swiss Re has set up a securitization programme called 'Vita Capital IV Ltd', which would allow it to receive up to $2bn in damages in the case of excess mortality linked to this type of disease. The French insurer Axa has a similar programme called 'Osiris Capital'. These are forms of collective life insurance that mutualize personal life insurance through the medium of securitization. Each time one of these programmes is put in place, insurers mount communications operations aimed at convincing investors of their preparedness faced with these pandemics, widely covered in the media.

Cat bonds were created in 1994. Since then, many hundreds have been issued, principally by insurers and reinsurers who wanted to protect themselves when faced with natural disasters that are too costly for classic insurance mechanisms to handle.[54] As we will see in a moment, states have also issued cat bonds, a fact not unrelated to the financial crisis they have been going through since the 1970s. In 2007 alone, twenty-seven cat bonds were issued, managing to raise more than $14bn. The average maturity of these bonds – that is, the period before their expiry, during which time interest accumulates – is three years. Cat bonds are a particular case of a more general category of bonds, *insurance-linked securities* (ILS), which are bonds linked to risks of various natures: credit, biotech, civil liability and so on. They are also labelled with the acronym ART, standing for alternative risk transfer. The first half of the 1990s was a turning point for the insurance industry. It was then that a series of unusually costly natural events, such as Hurricane Andrew in Florida in 1992, the Northridge, California earthquake in 1994 and the Kobe earthquake in Japan in 1995, all occurred within a very short period of time, thus compelling the industry to find new resources.

Not all the effects of climate change can be insured against. For example, desertification or rising sea levels cannot in themselves be the object of insurance coverage. The reason for this is that it is not possible to locate these phenomena spatially or temporally – this being the very condition of insurability. They are gradual rather than one-off and, in varying degrees, they concern the whole planet. Conversely, this type of phenomenon can interact with other phenomena and give rise to catastrophes that are insurable. Thus desertification contributes to the proliferation of droughts and the destruction of harvests, which can be covered by insurance.

A bond works in the following manner: some authority – an insurer, a reinsurer, a state – issues a bond through an investment bank; a bond which this latter sells to investors. As with any bond, the authority in question pays interest to these investors, in exchange for the money that they loan it. If catastrophe occurs, then the investors lose their money (the principal), which serves to reimburse those affected, or more precisely, the insurers and reinsurers who themselves reimburse those affected. If it does not take place, the investor pockets the interest. More accurately, the entity that issues a cat bond creates an *ad hoc* company called a *special purpose vehicle* (SPV). This company – which will typically be located in a tax haven – sets out in search of investors, placing the amounts that they lend it in bonds. If there is a catastrophic trigger event, then the principal and the profits emerging from the investment go to the issuing authority. Several types of event can trigger this process. It can be an event of a certain kind, damages that exceed some pre-determined threshold, a rapid series of events (for example, three cyclones hitting the same area within a brief time-frame) . . . As we can see, the cat bond has a structure very similar to that of the *respondentia* loans mentioned at the beginning of this chapter. The companies specialized in setting up cat bonds include Goldman Sachs Asset Management, Credit Suisse Asset Management, Axa Investment Managers . . .

Like all financial securities, cat bonds are evaluated by ratings agencies such as – mainly – Standard and Poor's as well as Fitch and Moody's. These bonds are generally rated BB, meaning that they are not without risk (as we know, AAA is the least risky bond rating, for example it applies to bonds issued by the German treasury). The value of a cat bond fluctuates on the market in function of the greater or lesser probability of catastrophe occurring and in function of the supply and demand for the relevant security. Sometimes these bonds continue to be exchanged even at the moment that the catastrophe is underway, or as catastrophe approaches, for example during a heatwave in Europe or as a hurricane approaches Florida. That is what traders who specialize in this domain call – with their characteristic way with words – 'live cat bond trading', meaning the exchange of cat bonds as a catastrophe plays out.[55]

There is a cat bonds exchange located in New Jersey called 'Catex' (Catastrophe Risk Exchange), which first appeared in 1995.[56] This exchange allows investors to diversify their risks. An investor who is overly exposed to earthquakes in California – that is, he has a portfolio whose excess of bonds in this field would cause it to go bust if an earthquake occurred in that state – can diversify his portfolio by exchanging his California cat bonds for ones covering hurricanes in the Caribbean or tsunamis in the Indian Ocean. Catex also has the function of providing its clients with databases of information allowing them to evaluate the level of catastrophic risks. There also exist other systems for pricing cat bonds. Swiss Re has also set up a 'Swiss Re cat bond index' making it possible to evaluate cat bonds' performance by comparison to the Standard and Poor's (S&P) 500, a stock price index of 500 major US companies.[57] For its part, the financial advice agency Artemis.bm, which specializes in cat bonds and is based in the tax haven Bermuda (where a major part of all worldwide insurance activity is concentrated), has an exhaustive list of the cat bonds issued since this financial product was first created.[58]

What advantages do cat bonds offer as compared to traditional insurance? Financial markets' capacity to absorb financial shocks is greatly superior to the insurance and reinsurance sectors' combined ability to do so. The total sums devoted to insurance and reinsurance in the world today are estimated at 350 to 400 billion dollars; a volume with a historic tendency to increase, even if economic crises are liable occasionally to affect this sector. But the bond market in the United States alone amounts to more than 29 trillion dollars,[59] and global stock market capitalization is over 60 trillion dollars. This is beyond comparison with the size of the insurance market. So, while an event like Katrina that costs 100 billion dollars or more is likely to cause serious danger to the traditional insurance market, for the financial markets it represents only a very small blip. Such an event corresponds to a 0.5 per cent fluctuation – a normal, everyday 'bearish' turn in these markets' volatility. The financialization of climatic risks is, then, (partly) the consequence of the increased cost of climate catastrophes.

What is investors' interest in investing in climate bonds? Mainly, risk diversification. Natural risks are not correlated with other sorts of risk: foreign exchange risk, fluctuations in raw material prices, in companies' shares . . . In times of crisis like today, this diversification is of considerable importance. It can, of course, be the case that a catastrophe will have a negative effect on the shares of a company whose headquarters is located where it takes place. But in principle cat bonds and other natural bonds do make up part of investors' strategies of diversifying their portfolios. Since the European sovereign debt crisis broke out in 2010, investors have been buying cat bonds in great numbers. The first quarter of 2011 was the most prolific in this market's history, with more than one billion dollars invested.[60] As one market operator explains, 'the debt crisis provided a demonstration of the diversification allowed by cat bonds and their lack of correlation with other financial markets. This sector has systematically realized good profits and proven its lack of volatility. More and more capital is being attracted to it.'

Nature as 'real abstraction'

Financial modelling agencies are a crucial actor in the cat bonds mechanism. These agencies devote their efforts to catastrophe modelling. Their objective, in short, is to calculate nature. As we have said, the characteristic of the new risks in general, and climate risks in particular, is their underlying uncertainty, meaning both the difficulty in predicting their occurrence and the difficulty in evaluating their cost if they do take place. Traditional bonds, for example state treasury bonds, fluctuate only slowly, which makes them fairly reliable securities whose evolution can be predicted. Cat bonds are much more difficult to predict, given the complexity of the – both natural and social – factors that have to be taken into account and the fact that catastrophes usually take place without warning. This is the reason why issuing such bonds always requires the involvement of modellers, whose goal is, indeed, to reduce the degree of uncertainty as far as possible. There are a small number of risk-modelling companies worldwide, most of them in the United States. The main ones are AIR (Applied Insurance Research), Eqecat and RMS (Risk Management Solutions).[61] These agencies develop models – and we will examine one specific example in a moment – in order to determine the probability of a natural event occurring and calculate its physical characteristics: wind speed, a cyclone's diameter, temperatures. These models also take into account the characteristics of the buildings and material assets of the implicated area: the materials used, the type of terrain, the risk reduction practices that have been implemented . . . The impact and cost of a catastrophe are, of course, closely linked to these factors. The combination of all this information makes it possible to estimate the cost of a catastrophe and the indemnities that the insurers would have to pay out and, consequently, to determine the price of a cat bond. The algorithms developed by these modellers are very mathematically sophisticated, reflecting the complexity of practices in the world of finance today. The modellers make use of methods like 'simulation' and 'counter-history', randomly generating virtual disasters so as to create a representation of their consequences and thus foresee these catastrophes in advance.[62]

These agencies frequently employ scientists who have come from the natural sciences in order to help them construct their models.[63] The Bermuda-based company Nephila Capital Limited[64] has thus made use of collaboration with oceanographers in order to model hurricanes in the Caribbean. With the help of climatologists and historians, Eqecat has created a database containing all the known catastrophes in the United States of the last three hundred years, as well as all those that have taken place in Europe over the last fifty years.[65] This recourse to both natural and social history is one of the means that allow them to get rid of part of the uncertainty linked to catastrophes and to assign natural risks a price.

These risk-modelling companies do not only model climatic risks. They model all types of risk, including terrorist attacks – and particularly so after 11 September 2001. The AIR and RMS agencies have, for example, hired former CIA and FBI agents in order to help evaluate the impact of such attacks.[66] These former agents' purpose is to inform these companies about the probability of fresh attacks on US soil and what their likely cost will be – also taking into account the location where they are committed. It seems that the models devoted to climate catastrophes have inspired the ones regarding terrorism. The firms developing these latter models had initially specialized in climate risk. Moreover, the climate and terrorism models now interpenetrate one another, given that certain models focused on terrorism also take into account the power and direction of the winds that will contribute to spreading chemical or biological agents across a population.[67] Taking notice of this interpenetration, the US insurer AIG has sold portfolios combining cover for all types of risk into a single financial product.[68]

The importance of modelling to cat bonds' functioning expresses a mechanism that is crucial to the formation of capitalist value: abstraction. This process corresponds to what Marxists call 'real abstractions', to which Marx referred in the *Grundrisse* when he wrote that 'individuals are now ruled by *abstractions*, whereas earlier they depended on one another'.[69] The specificity of capitalist forms of domination owes precisely to their being based on a mechanism of abstraction. Conversely, in pre-capitalist societies, domination is more immediate and individuals are 'dependent on one another', as Marx puts it. For his part, Alfred Sohn-Rethel defined the real abstraction as an abstraction 'other than by thought'; to put that another way, an abstraction that is the product, or responds to a need, of capital accumulation.[70] In a real abstraction, the object and its appearance become somehow indistinguishable and acquire a causal power of their own. How? If commodities are going to be exchanged on a market, they have to be commensurable – it has to be possible to assign them a price. This is the old problem of the passage from use-value to exchange-value; in other terms, the transformation of no-matter-what object into a commodity. Capitalism here runs into a sizeable obstacle: for use-value is singular and makes up part of the realm of quality, whereas exchange-value instead supposes that commodities are set in equivalence, with a view to their being exchanged; or, to put that another way, exchange-value is a matter of quantity. The history of capitalism is but a succession of measures seeking to overcome this obstacle and constantly to commodify new sectors of reality. And in this case, it is nature that it is being made commensurable.

In order to transcend the singularity of use-values, capitalism has to set in motion three powerful operations for (re) constructing reality. Firstly, it has to construct the object – that is, to delimit its contours precisely. A commodity does not exist in a natural state, as a commodity. It can only be exchanged once it has been *made* into a commodity. Secondly, it is necessary to 'disembed' the object, isolating it from its context. The – material and human – environment in which an object is inscribed is what gives it its singularity, which in the last instance is nothing other than the ensemble of relations that it entertains with the entities around it. In this sense, 'disembedding' means de-singularizing an object in order to set it in equivalence. The notion of 'disembedding' appears in Karl Polanyi's *The Great Transformation*, designating the process by which capitalism separates the market from its social substrate.

Finally, the passage from use-value to exchange-value requires the establishment of a generalized calculability; or, to put that another way, mathematical operations that signal to economic actors in what proportions commodities should be exchanged with one another. This consideration is vital for understanding the importance of the risk-modelling companies that we just mentioned. These three operations are precisely what Marxists call the 'real abstraction'. This real abstraction is typical of the capitalist system, conferring upon it the very particular form of domination characteristic of this mode of production.[71] Today we are witnessing a 'model-driven commodification'.[72] This expression designates the manner in which more and more sophisticated mathematical models underpin the commodification of new entities in contemporary capitalism. One among the best known of these models is the so-called 'Black–Scholes' formula, for which Robert Merton and Myron Scholes received the Nobel Prize in Economic Sciences in 1997. This formula concerns derivative products and is supposed to explain – and thus predict – the relation between a derivative and its 'underlying': that is, precisely the thing that the price of the derivative is derived from, be that a raw material, sovereign debt, the climate, etc. The question of to what extent this type of formula represents – or on the contrary, constructs – the reality that it is meant to explain is a complex one.[73] Their performative dimension is evident, as is the fact that they respond to an objective need of capitalism's: the formation of exchange-value. 'Derivative nature' is an expression sometimes used to refer to the manner in which the financialization process (re)constructs nature by modelling it.[74]

Carbon markets and unequal development

No case better illustrates these operations of capitalist value formation than 'carbon markets', or markets for pollution rights. These – along with intellectual property on the Internet – today count among 'the new enclosures' undergoing accelerated privatization, whose fundamental operation is equivalent to the enclosure of the 'commons' in seventeenth and eighteenth-century England. Carbon markets are based on two main mechanisms, namely the 'cap and trade' system for greenhouse gases, and the 'carbon offset' system.[75] The state or some other public authority (the UN, the European Union, etc.) sets an enterprise an emissions ceiling for CO_2 (or some other greenhouse gas), which it must not exceed. This ceiling is set lower than its past emissions, in order to compel the company to reduce them. If it does exceed this limit, it will pay the difference. The unit of accounting and exchange on the carbon markets, the 'carbon credit', is equivalent to one tonne of carbon. Its price fluctuates according to the trends of the market as well as the greater or lesser ambition of the state's chosen greenhouse gas reduction strategy. If the enterprise has emitted less than the predicted amount of 'carbon credits', it can sell them on the pollution rights market and thus pocket the advantage.

The pollution rights trading system with the greatest volume, worldwide, is the 'European Union emission trading system' (EU ETS). The EU ETS is aimed at achieving the greenhouse gas reduction targets to which the EU committed in the Kyoto Protocol. The Chicago Climate Exchange, created in 2003, is the oldest such exchange. According to the World Bank, the pollution rights market at the global scale rose from a volume of $10bn in 2005 to $144bn in 2009, with the crisis subsequently stabilizing it at around $142bn.[76] It is difficult to get a clear view of the trend of a market of such pronounced opacity, since the rules that govern its functioning have still not been clearly established. The volume of transactions on the carbon markets is partly sustained by speculative activity; namely, intervention in these markets by financial intermediaries who do not themselves need to reduce their emissions, but who buy and sell credits on the secondary market in order to pocket the profits. These 'climate entrepreneurs' and the speculation in which they engage amounts to more than a third of all transactions.[77]

Since it was first established, the European pollution rights market has faced serious problems in regulating supply and demand. Under the influence of industrial interests, the carbon credits were initially handed out too generously, which meant that the price of the credits was very low and, therefore, that companies were not incentivized to reduce their emissions so as then to be able to sell their pollution rights on the market. This over-allocation of permits today gives firms the possibility not only of continuing to pollute just like before, but even of increasing their profits along the way by selling the credits that the state has so generously allotted to them. Reducing the volume of credits in circulation in order to push up the price would require courageous political decisions, at a continent-wide level. We should also note that in decreasing growth rates, the economic crisis that began in 2007–8 thereby also reduced CO_2 emissions.

In addition to this credits-based mechanism, there is another system based on 'carbon offsetting'. An enterprise can redeem its 'ecological debt' – its excess greenhouse gas emissions – by investing in projects that help reduce such emissions elsewhere in the world, in particular in developing regions. This allows enterprises or countries to finance the preservation of the environment and, moreover, the construction of hydroelectric dams (counting for more than 25% of these offset projects) generating a supposedly 'clean' energy in order to avoid having to reduce their emissions.[78] The underlying idea is that it is easier and more effective to take measures to introduce non-polluting energy sources in developing countries, than to try to reduce emissions in already developed ones. This offset mechanism exists today not only in the domain of pollution rights but also, for example, with regard to preserving biodiversity; if it is lost or damaged in one location, that can be offset by improvements in other locations, following certain conditions.

The pollution rights markets perfectly illustrate the process of commodification mentioned above. In these markets we see the three operations that we earlier highlighted: construction, disembedding and calculability. The emergence of carbon markets firstly supposes the construction of a quota – the tonne of carbon or 'credit' – that serves as a unit of accounting and exchange. There is nothing 'natural' about this, even if the gases themselves are; after all, as we can imagine, this value could be categorized in any number of different ways. This entity is then disembedded – that is, made independent of its context. It is this disembedding that allows for processes playing out on opposite sites of the planet – for example, a polluting French company financing (supposedly) ecologically clean projects in Asia – to be considered commensurable. The implication of this offsetting mechanism is that pollution in France and the construction of a hydroelectric dam in Asia are ecological equivalents – in all regards, an absurd statement – and its condition of possibility is a powerful mechanism of disembedding and abstraction.

The offsetting system follows – and also reinforces – the contours of unequal development on the worldwide scale.[79] As such, the emissions resulting from the production of commodities made outside Europe, but imported to within its borders, are not counted as European emissions. In this sense, the offshoring of production tends to reduce emissions in a merely mechanical sense, as well as reducing labour-power costs (of course) for the multinationals concerned. To put it another way, the more 'global value chains' extend, the more production is globalized (the more it profits from unequal development) and the more difficult it is to identify and control the source of emissions. 'Imported emissions' is a term sometimes used to designate these emissions that have not been accounted for.

All this is possible thanks to mathematical modelling. But, as well as private firms – banks, ratings agencies, brokers specialized in environmental bonds such as Eko Asset Management or Inflection Point Asset Management – another very important actor allows the commodification of nature: the state. Both nation-states and supranational bodies play a crucial role in the emergence of these markets, because it is the state that sets in place the socio-technical mechanism and the accounting systems that allow them to function; it is the state that fixes the quotas for the different enterprises and sectors; and so on. The state's role as an interface between capitalism and nature is thus clearly apparent in the example of these carbon markets. State, capitalism and nature are a triptych that we ought to think through in conjunction, in the context of the environmental crisis.

Constructing profitable markets

When disasters occur, insurers tend to put up insurance premiums, sometimes raising them to prohibitive prices. This produces exclusionary effects, with the excessive premiums disincentivizing individuals from taking out insurance. This, in turn, shrinks the market and forces the insurers to increase their premiums still further on account of insufficient demand.

This problem is particularly acute in poor countries. The existence of an insurance market supposes the presence of a sufficient number of people who have the means available to take out insurance; otherwise, the risks would be insufficiently diversified and the insurers would therefore be unable to pay out in the event of catastrophe. In developing countries

this minimum threshold is rarely reached. Moreover, sometimes it is also the case that the legal framework in such
countries is defective; and the emergence of an insurance
market in the absence of a stable legal framework certainly
raises problems. The securitization of climate risks is a way
for insurance companies and governments to get around these
obstacles.

The World Food Programme (WFP) has thus issued a
climate security – a derivative, not a bond (we will return to
this distinction in a moment) – for the benefit of the Ethiopian
government, so that it can support its population in the case
of droughts and lost harvests.[80] Ethiopia is prey to recurrent
droughts, which are aggravated by climate change. They give
rise to famines, which the Ethiopian government does not
have the means to handle and which the humanitarian aid
sector often instead takes charge of. This is a form of insurance called 'index-based insurance'; the words 'index-based'
indicate that its trigger mechanism is a graded scale, for
example a scale of temperature or of rainfall, with the indemnity being paid out when a certain threshold is reached. Insurance systems of this kind also exist in Bolivia, India and Sudan
and they are actively promoted by international organizations. They make up part of 'microinsurance', a system that
is burgeoning at the present moment and which represents the
insurance sector's equivalent of microcredit.[81] Microinsurance
is symptomatic of the *financialization of daily life* that is currently at work.[82] The proliferation of natural disasters, which
owes to climate change, promises this sector a bright future.

As its name suggests, microinsurance involves small
amounts of money and poor populations – but ones who risk
incurring major losses due to natural disasters. As in the case
of microcredit, it is managed in a communal manner, in the
sense that responsibility for paying the premiums is collectively controlled. Microinsurance concerns various different
hazards: health, harvests or livestock perishing, flooding . . .
and it today covers between 150 and 200 million people.
Munich Re has published several volumes devoted to micro-
insurance in collaboration with the International Labor
Organization (ILO).[83] This collaboration between public and
private – in this case, international organizations – is a constant element of the insurance sector. The stated goal, as

always, is to protect the poorest; but raking in the premiums (even if they are microscopic) paid by millions of poor peasants around the world is certainly not alien to the interests of the world's number one reinsurer for this sector. Microinsurance can be considered a sophisticated form of 'accumulation by dispossession', in David Harvey's sense of the term.[84] Again, we are dealing with the same principle: in a period in which the rate of profit is declining, how can sectors of social life and the population that had hitherto escaped the market's grip, now be made profitable?

Profitability is a political construct. The international organizations which operate in the field of development have for around a decade been working with private enterprises in developing 'market models for the poor'.[85] Such a course of action is inscribed within the ideology of the 'empowerment' of the poor, seeking to get them to take control over their own existence. Microcredit and microinsurance start out from this approach. The method here implemented seeks to make sectors of the population who lack the means to be integrated into the market – because they are too poor – into creditworthy ones. This requires that two conditions be fulfilled. Firstly, the markets for the poor have to be arranged on a massive scale, involving millions of individuals. The amount that an Indian or Bolivian peasant can afford to pay as an insurance premium is extremely low. Next, the aggregate sum of premiums that the insurers collect must be enough for them to be able to cover for diseases and disasters, while at the same time pocketing a profit. The conclusion: there has to be a huge amount of premiums. It is the fact that the countries to which these market models are applied are very highly populated that makes such an operation not only feasible, but financially lucrative for the insurers.

The integration of the poor into the insurance market moreover often requires state subsidies of insurance premiums, at least to start with. This is the so-called 'public–private partnership' mechanism, or PPP. This is one of the pillars of the neoliberal insurance regime and we today find manifestations of it in all sectors of the economy, for example in school building or prison management. In 2011, Swiss Re published a report entitled 'Closing the financial gap. New partnerships between the public and the private sectors to finance disaster risks'.[86] The financial 'gap' to which the title refers is the gap separating poor peasants in developing countries from insurability – meaning, profitability for the insurers. According to Swiss Re, it is up to the state to bridge this 'gap', driving the poor peasant or the inhabitant of the planet of slums towards the market, so that insurers can insure him. The Swiss reinsurer advances several arguments in order to convince states of this. For example, it argues that an uninsured peasant is less productive. Subject to the vicissitudes of nature or illness, he will tend to invest less in equipment and fertilizers, leading to stagnation in his productivity. Moreover, in the last instance he will be a charge on the state, since if his harvest is destroyed or he falls ill he will look to the state for help. Swiss Re gives this as the reason why the state should make such private insurance compulsory. So-called 'sovereign' cat bonds, which are issued by states in partnership with private insurers, are one of the means by which these public–private partnerships are tied. As Michel Foucault has shown, neoliberalism has little to do with '*laissez-faire*' and everything to do with permanent state intervention in favour of the markets.

The insurer's own country of origin may sometimes intervene in the implementation of insurance systems in developing countries. For example, *Direction du développement et de la coopération* (DDC), a branch of the Swiss foreign ministry, actively supports Swiss Re in these countries.[87] In particular, it tries to make sure that the legal framework for insurance law develops in a manner favourable to the reinsurer. Switzerland is particularly active in 'Helvétistan'.[88] This expression designates the group of countries that it represents at the IMF and the World Bank, international organizations whose governance is arranged on the basis of poor countries' interests (supposedly) being represented by a rich one.[89] This group comprises most of the countries of Central Asia, including Tajikistan, Kazakhstan, Turkmenistan, Kyrgyzstan and Uzbekistan, whose names end in 'stan', hence 'Helvétistan'.

A 'multi-cat' bond in Mexico

Thus far, most cat bonds have been issued by insurers and reinsurers who want to protect themselves from catastrophes.

However, since the mid 2000s a tendency has emerged for states also to issue these securities. This is what theorists of insurance call 'sovereign' cat bonds, much as we speak of 'sovereign' debt.[90] This tendency is actively encouraged by international organizations operating in the economic field, first among them the World Bank and the OECD. The United Nations also has a risk reduction secretariat, created in 1999, which has deployed a *United Nations international strategy for disaster reduction* (UNISDR).[91] This approach was originally developed by a group of contemporary insurance theorists, many of them based at the Wharton School of the University of Pennsylvania, which is one of the world's most prestigious business schools. It is also home to a research institute called the Risk Management and Decision Processes Center, which is at the forefront of analysing the theoretical questions that underpin the insurance of climatic risks.[92]

In 2006 Mexico issued a cat bond allowing it to cover itself for earthquakes. In 2009 the country decided to include hurricanes in this same mechanism, thus giving rise to a 'multi-cat' programme; namely, one that covers a multiple number of potential catastrophes.[93] Mexico is vulnerable to numerous hazards, both natural and otherwise. These include hurricanes, of course – particularly in the Gulf of Mexico region – but also earthquakes, landslides and also volcanic activity, for example Popocatépetl, a volcano that overlooks Mexico City, which has recently become active again. The 8.1 magnitude earthquake that struck Mexico in September 1985 claimed more than 10,000 dead and 30,000 wounded, with the damage being estimated at some $5bn. And we should not forget the fact that since the 1990s Mexico has been in a situation of latent civil war on account of the growing power of narco-trafficking, absorbing a significant portion of the means of a country cruelly lacking in resources.

In Mexico, as elsewhere, the state is the insurer of last resort in the event of natural disaster. The indemnification of the victims is paid out of the state budget, meaning that in the last instance it comes from taxation, on the basis of a principle of national solidarity consubstantial with the modern nation-state. This is the same principle that prevails in sectors like healthcare or pension provision in certain countries. The growing power of the humanitarian sector from the last quarter of the twentieth century onward complements this state mechanism with a private one, managed by NGOs. This latter support is often proportional to the extent that the disaster rouses an emotional response among international public opinion. International organizations like the World Bank and United Nations Development Programme (UNDP) will also likely intervene.

The large number of natural disasters in Mexico led the government to set up a Natural Disasters Fund (*Fondo de desastres naturales*; 'FONDEN'). The fund makes both short and long-term interventions: it provides emergency financial aid to the victims in the first moments following a catastrophe and after that it finances the rebuilding of infrastructure. FONDEN is a legally independent fund, but is financed by the state budget. Up until the early 2000s the system worked properly, given the relatively low cost of the natural disasters it faced. However, a series of exorbitantly costly disasters then struck the country. That was why in 2005, for example, a federal government that had predicted that it would have to devote $50m to disaster relief instead ended up spending $800m.[94]

It was in this context that the idea of securitizing Mexico's climate disaster insurance saw the light of day. Working under the auspices of the World Bank, which played the role of 'global coordinator', the lead agents of the 'multi-cat' programme set in motion a cycle of meetings and negotiations. Only serious players got a seat at the table: the Mexican finance minister as well as Goldman Sachs and Swiss Re Capital Markets, who were charged with selling the programme to investors. Munich Re was also a stakeholder, as were two major US law firms, namely Cadwalader, Wickersham & Taft and White & Case. The risk-modelling agency responsible for setting the terms of this cat bond's trigger mechanism was Applied Insurance Research (AIR). It developed two distinct models, one for earthquakes and one for hurricanes, each time specifying the geographic location of the event (and for hurricanes, their trajectories) and its physical characteristics. In the first case, that meant their magnitude on the Richter scale and their depth, and in the latter case the wind speeds concerned.

Once Goldman Sachs and Swiss Re had registered the cat bond in the Cayman Islands, in the form of a special purpose vehicle, it was sold to investors by way of 'road shows' – this being the name for the presentation of a financial product new to the market – organized by the banks. Each time a disaster strikes Mexico, the AIR agency calculates whether it corresponds to the parameters established by the contracting parties and thus allows for a financial sum to be made available. For instance, when the state of Baja California was affected by an earthquake in April 2010, particularly the towns of Calexico and Mexicali, its epicentre was to the north of the area delimited by the cat bond;[95] in consequence, the bond money was not released and Mexico continued paying interest. Similarly, a hurricane struck the state of Tamaulipas in 2010, but it was less powerful than the pre-determined threshold and so here again the money was not released. Frequently when a disaster strikes it leads to negotiations. In 1999 there were long debates among insurers and the insured over the question of whether the Lothar and Martin hurricanes that had swept across France constituted two hurricanes or just one.[96] The insurers insisted that this was just one climate event, so that they would not have to pay out indemnities twice.

Sovereign cat bonds are also being set up in Asia, as a late 2011 ASEAN dossier reveals.[97] ASEAN is the Association of Southeast Asian Nations: it includes Thailand, Indonesia, Malaysia, Singapore, the Sultanate of Brunei, Vietnam, Burma, Cambodia, Laos and the Philippines. This region is highly exposed to natural disasters and climate change will probably increase yet further the number and power of the disasters still to come. To the extent that some of these ASEAN countries are Muslim – Indonesia is the world's largest Muslim country – it is the principles of Islamic insurance, *takaful*, that apply, here. We can note in passing that today Islamic insurance is experiencing 25 per cent annual growth, while in recent years the traditional insurance market has grown by an average of 10 per cent.[98] Swiss Re is thus making a lot of effort to strengthen what it calls its 'Sharia Credibility'.

The insurance system that this ASEAN report recommends operates at three levels. The first concerns risks that are recurrent but of little extent, such as local floods or land-slides. In this case, funds come out of the state budget: the report suggests specific funding envelopes dedicated to this purpose. The financial sums at stake here are sometimes significant ones, but not sufficiently so as to endanger a state's financial stability. The second level, which concerns earth-quakes or more major flooding, calls for 'contingent credit' from the World Bank. The World Bank issues 'Catastrophic Risk Deferred Drawdown Options'.[99] These options allow a country to receive rapid financial aid in the event of a disaster. Like any other loan from the World Bank, they come with strings attached. Beyond paying interest, a country claiming such funding has to implement 'a hazard risk measurement programme',[100] notably including the development of part-nerships with the private sector and must encourage the emer-gence of private markets to handle catastrophic risks. These contingent credits can amount to up to $500m. The third level concerns infrequent risks that have disastrous conse-quences: major earthquakes, tropical cyclones, tsunamis, etc. This is the level for high finance: given the costs that these disasters induce, only this type of funding is liable to dealing with them.

Mexico and these Asian countries are not the only ones to have set up sovereign cat bonds. Turkey, Chile and even the US state of Alabama, hit hard by Hurricane Katrina in 2005, have also done so, in one form or another.

Ecological crisis and the fiscal crisis of the state

The state financialization of the insurance for climate disas-ters has a deeper cause, and an examination of this theme will allow us to set ecological questions in relation with capi-talism and its crises. One objective of the Mexican 'multi-cat' programme – as even those who conceived it openly confess – is to 'protect the public finances' of the issuing country, or, indeed, to 'immunise their fiscal policy'.[101] The ASEAN report, for its part, speaks of strengthening its member coun-tries' 'financial resilience', 'protecting the long-term fiscal balance' by financializing the insurance for climate risks.

These bond programmes were finalized in 2009, at the very time that the gravest crisis of capitalism since the Great Depression of the 1930s was raging. A characteristic of the current crisis is the immense increase in sovereign debts; that is to say, the indebtedness of the states at the centre of the world economy, the USA and Europe first among them. This indebtedness is the fruit of massive tax cuts – of neoliberal inspiration – for the richest; a significant fall in tax revenue due to the slowdown of growth; and the state bailouts of banks and other financial institutions at the moment of crisis. The sovereign debt crisis has emerged in the context of what some authors, including James O'Connor and Wolfgang Streeck, have called 'the fiscal crisis of the state'. This expression refers to the fact that states no longer have the financial means to pay for their policies and that this is no passing phenomenon but a structural one, emerging since the last quarter of the twentieth century. This structural fact has been further aggravated by the sovereign debt crisis.

According to Streeck, states are today faced with two mutually contradictory obligations. On the one hand, to consolidate their public finances. This would allow them to borrow at lower interest rates than they are currently doing, as the markets force them to reduce their deficits and debt. On the other hand, to continue to provide high levels of public investment in education, healthcare, pensions, etc., since populations' expectations in terms of their welfare have constantly increased, at least since the end of the Second World War. In a period of historically low growth rates, which has endured for several decades, these two obligations are irreconcilable. This is what leads Streeck – taking his cue from O'Connor, on this point – to state that capitalism will not much longer be compatible with democracy.

The fiscal crisis of the state is closely linked to the environmental crisis. Given the fiscal crisis that states are going through, they are less and less capable of taking on the insurance cost of climate disasters through conventional means, which principally means taxation. They will be even less able to do so as the number and power of these disasters increases due to climate change. That is the point where ecological crisis and financial crisis fuse. That is true for every part of the world, but particularly so for the most fragile states.

Developing countries are often the ones hardest hit by climate disasters, not only because these are the areas where such catastrophes take place, but also because the means that they have at hand for dealing with them are much lower than what developed countries possess. Rising sea levels affect the Netherlands just as much as Bangladesh, yet it is evidently preferable to be confronted with this situation in the former rather than the latter country. The Caribbean island of Grenada provides an instructive case, in this sense. This island was struck by Hurricane Ivan in 2004, when it was already indebted to 90 per cent of GDP. Considering its existing debt levels it was incapable of meeting the expenses that it incurred through this disaster, and was forced to declare a default the following year.

The financial crisis drives states increasingly to financialize the insurance for climate risks, with securitization considered an alternative to taxation and national solidarity. The fiscal crisis of the state, the environmental crisis and financialization are thus three closely linked phenomena. This argument can be generalized. Originally, there was little or no cost to exploiting nature. Over time, however, the resources that are being exhausted become more expensive; and simultaneously, managing the harmful effects of development – the fight against pollution, costs linked to workers' health, nuclear accidents . . . – itself becomes increasingly costly. This tendency pushes down the rate of profit. So what does capitalism do? It transfers the growing cost of reproducing the conditions of production to the state. This is the system's very logic: socialization of costs, privatization of profits. The rise in the costs relating to the conditions of production plunges the state into a fiscal crisis. Tax revenues do not increase at the same rhythm as expenditure – all the more so given that since the 1970s the growth rate of long-developed countries has been depressed. For this reason, there is a structural deficit in the public finances.

The fiscal crisis of the state leads it to borrow ever more from the financial markets, in order to finance its expenditure and investment and fictitiously re-establish a balance in its accounts. This is one of the causes of the financialization of capital.[102] An important factor in this financialization is the rising expense of the conditions of production and the growing costs generated by the exploitation of nature. Capitalism exploits nature, which leads to ever greater costs for the state, which turns to the finance markets in order to be able to cope.

The fiscal crisis and the environmental crisis also interact in other ways. As we have seen, one characteristic of the new risks is hypercorrelation, meaning that they affect entire regions. A disaster disrupts economic activity in a certain area in a lasting manner. This can lead to a slowdown in growth, which in turn decreases tax revenues, since these are proportional to growth. Moreover, this slowdown obliges the state to spend more in terms of unemployment insurance and other forms of social security. An ecological crisis that proliferates disasters is thus liable to aggravating the fiscal crisis considerably. Climate change may create even more indirect costs for social security and health systems. Because of global warming, pathogenic agents are appearing in regions that had previously been free of them.[103] For example, with rising temperatures, a growing part of US territory risks becoming exposed to malaria. This type of risk will doubtless engender extra health expenditure, further deepening the fiscal crisis of the state.

A derivative nature

Cat bonds and carbon credits are not the only financial products plugged into natural processes; far from it. Weather derivatives are another such product. Swaps, calls and puts are examples of derivatives. Climate derivatives do not concern natural disasters, but rather the weather of the moment. They have to do with variations that are not catastrophic in scope and which do not interrupt the normal course of social life when they are triggered. From sporting events and harvests affected by hailstorms, to rock concerts and fluctuating gas prices, plenty of aspects of modern life are influenced by weather. It is estimated that 25 per cent of developed countries' GDP is exposed to the impact of climatic variations.[104] A climate derivative releases a financial sum when temperatures – or some other climate variable – are higher or lower than some medium level, for example if the cold (and thus the cost of energy) exceeds certain limits, or if rain reduces attendance at an amusement park in summer. In the agricultural domain, some derivatives' 'underlying' is the time that it takes for plants to germinate. The 'growing degree days' index measures the gap between the average (mean) temperature that it takes for a harvest to ripen and the real temperature, triggering payment if a certain threshold is exceeded. In a 'swap', two enterprises that the variations in the climate will affect in opposite ways can agree to insure one another. If an energy company loses money in the event of a winter that is too mild and a company organizing sports events will lose money if it is too harsh, one will pay the other a predetermined sum depending on whether it is mild or harsh.[105] The ancestors of climate derivatives appeared in nineteenth-century agriculture, more particularly in the Chicago Board of Trade in the United States, and were concerned with raw materials like cotton and wheat. With the 1970s liberalization and decompartmentalization of the finance markets and the proliferation of derivative products that followed, the potential forms of 'underlying' multiplied. Energy multinationals including Enron were pioneers in this field. In 1998–99, a particularly mild winter in the US on account of the La Niña phenomenon led to major losses for these companies, which accelerated the growth in the importance of derivatives, through which intermediary these companies 'smooth out' their risk of losses. [106] Variations of even just a few degrees are of truly colossal financial importance to these companies. Starting in 1999 climate derivatives were exchanged on the Chicago Mercantile Exchange, which has historically specialized in agricultural products. The emergence of climate derivatives goes hand-in-hand with the growing tendency for meteorological services to be privatized, notably in the Anglo-Saxon countries.[107] These services make up financial and political stakes of some significance, since it is they, in the last instance, who determine the thresholds beyond which a derivative is triggered.

The appearance of climate derivatives should be set in the more general context of the 'derivatives revolution' of the last third of the twentieth century, concomitant with the emergence of neoliberalism.[108] In the first half of the 1970s the

Bretton Woods system was abandoned. When exchange rates were floated again, governments and businesses had to cover themselves from the risk of unforeseen currency variations, directly linked to foreign trade and profits. Currency derivatives and later Treasury bond derivatives served precisely this purpose. This 'derivatives revolution' took place in Chicago, in the very same place that the first agricultural derivatives had been created, at the Chicago Board of Trade and the Chicago Mercantile Exchange. The *savoir-faire* relating to agricultural derivatives was thus repurposed, as derivatives concerning currency and other forms of 'underlying' were put in place.[109]

In an article entitled 'Why environmentalism needs high finance' three insurance theorists suggested setting up a 'species swap' – a form of derivative having to do with the risk of species becoming extinct.[110] Here, the interpenetration of finance and nature takes on one of its most radical forms. The idea is a simple one: it is a matter of making it profitable for businesses to preserve species, such as to incentivize them to take care of the endangered species found on their territory. Preservation is expensive and it is mostly state money that is mobilized to this purpose – funding that tends to run short in times of crisis. As we see, once again the fiscal crisis of the state is invoked as an argument justifying the financialization of nature. A species swap takes place between the state and a private enterprise. Let's imagine a threatened variety of tortoise in Florida, which lives in a company's waters. If the number of specimens increased because the enterprise takes care of them, the state pays it interest. In passing, this allows it to justify its nature preservation activities to its shareholders, since such activities thus become profitable. If, on the contrary, the number of specimens should decline, or approaches the brink of extinction, it is instead the company that pays money to the state, such that it can engage in an operation to save them. This mechanism is supposed to incentivize the private sector to take charge of preserving species and allow the state to devote less money to this activity.

Environmental mortgages (a sort of subprime, whose 'underlying' is not on the housing market, but rather part of the environment), forest-backed securities and mechanisms to indemnify wetlands, liberalized by the George H. W. Bush administration in the 1990s, are other examples of the same type of financial products.[111]

Nature as accumulation strategy

Capitalism, James O'Connor tells us, has 'conditions of production'. These conditions of production are not commodities, properly speaking, but they do allow for commodities to be produced. O'Connor is here taking his cue from Karl Polanyi, who called them 'fictitious commodities' in order to emphasize that even if they are considered commodities, their ontology is distinct from that of normal ones. 'Conditions of production' include, for example, labour, land or money. As capitalism develops, it exhausts and even destroys them. If for over a century the availability of oil – a fictitious commodity if there was one – at low prices allowed for what Timothy Mitchell calls 'carbon democracy',[112] its increasing scarcity makes this condition of production considerably more expensive. This upward pressure on the cost of the conditions of production – the fact that capitalism requires these conditions of production and yet is simultaneously unable to stop itself from exhausting them – is what O'Connor calls the 'second contradiction' of capitalism. If the 'first contradiction' opposes capital and labour, this second one opposes capital and nature.[113]

These two contradictions mutually feed one another. Insofar as human labour generates surplus-value – value – by transforming nature, it underwrites the identity between natural and social history; to put that another way, it guarantees that these two contradictions are interlinked. The first contradiction leads to a downward tendency in the rate of profit, meaning the emergence of profound crises in the capitalist system. The second, for its part, makes it increasingly costly to maintain the conditions of production. This also weighs down on profit rates, since the growing volumes of capitals employed in maintaining their supply – for example, the search for oil reserves, which are ever more difficult to access – are capitals not transformed into profits. The modern state should be conceived as the interface between capital and nature. It is the authority that regulates the usage of the conditions of production, in order that capital is able to exploit them. If nature were simply handed over to capital, without any interface, capital would rapidly destroy it. Capitalism needs the state first of all for reasons of self-limitation. As we have seen, it also needs it for the purposes of constructing nature. That is why the central question for any ecological movement worthy of the name is the question of the state.

Using a shorter timescale, we can also take a slightly different approach to this question. For capitalism, the environmental crisis is not only a problem, a factor weighing down the profit rate which it thus has to try to manage. This crisis can also be a genuine *accumulation strategy*.[114] As Gramsci demonstrated, crises are always ambivalent moments for capitalism: on the one hand, they represent a risk to the system's survival, but on the other hand, they also offer the prospect of generating new opportunities for making profits. The environmental crisis is also marked by this ambivalence. For example, Hurricane Katrina destroyed colossal volumes of capital. But it also allowed the emptying-out and making-profitable of what had previously been working-class – and thus unprofitable – neighbourhoods, and it also allowed the massive privatization of public services, including schools. The same was true of the 2004 tsunami in Asia, which led to the enclosure of numerous coastal regions and drew international hotel and restaurant chains to move into these areas. All the examples that we have mentioned in this chapter, from cat bonds to climate derivatives, via carbon markets and 'species swaps', bear witness to the manner in which capital draws profits from the environmental crisis that is now underway. So the crisis has not only had negative effects for capital; for it still also has the possibility of 'capitalizing on chaos'.[115] Fundamentally, this point of view does not stand in contradiction with James O'Connor's; they are different perspectives on one same phenomenon. In the short term, capitalism manages to draw profits from the crisis. But nonetheless, the constant pressure that it exerts on the conditions of production gives reason to believe that its very survival is now at stake.

Conclusion

Let's give a recap of the path we have travelled thus far. Industrial development – capitalism – is at the origin of environmental crisis and environmental inequalities. But in tandem with this, the system also produces 'antibodies' to deal with this crisis. Financialization is one of these antibodies. It protects investment from the consequences of climate change; cushions the resultant increase in the costs of the 'conditions of production'; and simultaneously provides an opportunity for profits, in a global context marked by a long-term economic crisis. Financialization is thus one of capitalism's first reactions faced with the ecological crisis.

Now we will turn to a second mechanism that allows the system a pre-emptive means of protecting itself from the effects of this crisis: namely, war. Given the increased inequalities to which this ecological crisis gives rise, it leads to armed conflicts of a new type. It brings about developments in the modalities of collective violence, which herald a new era in the history of war. As well as being financialized, then, the ecological crisis is being militarized. Moreover, militaries are themselves conscious of this development; in fact, for some years they have been integrating the consequences of climate change into their strategic analyses . . .

3

Green Wars, or the
Militarization of Ecology

[If] it is impossible to obtain exact information . . . a
general should never move without arranging several
courses of action for himself, based upon probable
hypotheses.

Antoine-Henri Jomini

The National Security Strategy (NSS) document signed by
Barack Obama in 2010 was the first to include a section
devoted to the military implications of climate change. Given
the impact of climate change upon the environment and on
populations, it is imperative for the US armed forces to integrate its consequences into their strategic calculations.[1] The
NSS is updated every five to ten years and the previous report
dated back to 2002, during George W. Bush's first term, just
after the 11 September 2001 attacks. This document had
included the doctrine of the 'preventative war', whose application in Iraq was now being prepared. In each period the
NSS report notes the major politico-military tendencies
playing out on the world scale: the end of the Cold War,
the emergence of 'terrorism' . . . but also the increase in oil
prices or the risks of pandemics. It allows the ruling classes
to determine the country's medium and long-term strategic
objectives. The publication of the NSS report is always preceded by debates on these themes, both within the ruling

administration and in the think tanks and journals associated with foreign policy, of which there are many on the East Coast.

In this vein, in the second half of the 2000s several expert commissions put together by these think tanks produced reports concerning the link between climate change and war. Most of these commissions included high-ranking officers (both retired and still active) from the various parts of the armed forces, from the Navy to the Army, Air Force and Coastguard. The think tanks in question included the Center for Naval Analysis, the Center for a New American Security, the Council on Foreign Relations, the Center for American Progress, the Brookings Institution and so on. The earliest of these dossiers date back to 2007. One of them was entitled 'The age of consequences. The foreign policy and national security implications of global climate change.' This report was jointly issued by the Center for Strategic and International Studies and the Center for a New American Security. The 'age of consequences' in question – a title referring to a speech by Winston Churchill, made upon the eve of the Second World War – was defined as the age that would see 'the intersection of climate change and the security of nations'.[2] The document outlined three possible scenarios for the twenty-first century: 'expected' climate change, with global temperatures increasing by 1.3°C by 2040; 'severe' climate change, with temperatures rising by 2.6°C, giving rise to 'non-linear' – that is, unpredictable – environmental events; and finally, a 'catastrophic' scenario based on temperatures increasing by 5.6°C by 2100, threatening nations' 'internal cohesion'.

The question of the link between war and climate change now frequently appears in the columns of *Armed Forces Journal*, the US military officers' monthly, and in *Foreign Affairs*, which expresses the prevalent diplomatic consensus in Washington. This was the publication in which George Kennan presented the 'containment doctrine' at the end of the 1940s and in which Samuel Huntington heralded the 'clash of civilizations' at the start of the 1990s. In 2009 the CIA founded a Center for Climate Change and National Security. Its task is to reflect on the effects that climate change has on 'national security' and to provide strategic information to the US negotiators taking part in international conferences on this question. In 2010 the *Quadriennial Defense Review* (*QDR*) published by the Pentagon had a chapter devoted to environmental change. This report is the most important document that the US Department of Defense produces with regard to military doctrine.

According to the *QDR*, climate change will affect the armed forces' various missions in several different ways. Increasing both the number and intensity of natural disasters, it will change the 'operational environment' in which militaries operate and will also have an impact on military installations and materiel. For example, the Pascagoula naval base in the state of Mississippi was heavily damaged by Hurricane Katrina and the repairs cost several billion dollars. Thirty US military bases around the world are already under threat from rising sea levels. One of the main US military hubs in the Indian Ocean is a base situated on the island of Diego Garcia, a stopping-off point for many ships and aircraft in transit to or from Asia. This base was a strategic hub during the Cold War and, with China's rising power, it has again taken on decisive importance in the US's military deployment. Yet Diego Garcia stands only a few metres above sea level and rising sea levels threaten to engulf it, perhaps around the middle of the twenty-first century.[3] The same is also true of the US base at Guam in the Pacific Ocean, which served as a runway for planes taking off to bomb Japan during the Second World War.

A doctrine emerges

While this body of doctrine crystallized over the course of the 2000s, US elites' first reflection on the military implications of climate change came rather earlier. The first report explicitly referring to this problem, which was ordered by Jimmy Carter, dates back to 1977.[4] The experts charged with looking into this problem included Thomas Schelling, a great contemporary game theorist, 2005 Nobel Prize economics laureate and one of the thinkers behind the US doctrine of 'nuclear dissuasion'. From that point onward Schelling has continued to make interventions regarding the question of climate change, from the perspective of its economic and geopolitical consequences.[5] He is a partisan of 'geo-engineering', namely the technological manipulation of the climate in order to combat global warming.[6] Even before that, the Pentagon organized a June 1947 meeting devoted to the military consequences of ice melting in the Arctic.[7] In the early 1990s Al Gore, who was at that time the vice-president, helped to breathe life back into reflection on this subject. A series of conferences also took place within NATO and from then onward this transatlantic organization was at the forefront of addressing this question. In 1993 it published a document entitled 'Environmental policy statement for the armed forces', designed to increase the alliance's soldiers' 'ecological awareness'.[8] In 2008, its Dutch general secretary Jaap de Hoop Scheffer declared environmental change one of the organization's new 'strategic horizons'. The following year his successor, former Danish prime minister Anders Fogh Rasmussen, argued that 'no single government can confront climate change on its own', since this is, by its very nature, a problem that transcends national boundaries. [9] It shares this characteristic with terrorism – for terrorist networks also span such borders – and thus it requires new modalities of international cooperation. For this reason, Rasmussen added, NATO could in future play a key role in managing climate change's effects on 'collective security'. After the end of the Cold War, the transatlantic organization sought a new *raison d'être*; and it seems to have found it.

The American military is not the only one interested in climate change – far from it. Over recent years, all the world's major armed forces have investigated the military consequences of this phenomenon, from Britain to China, Brazil, India, France, Australia and Canada. In 2010, one of the main journals of military thinking in France, the *Revue de défense nationale*, devoted a special issue to 'climate geostrategy' as well as the notion of 'natural security'. This dossier, with a preface by Michel Rocard,[10] featured articles with evocative titles such as 'When security goes green' and 'Climate: a matter of security or strategic control?' – this latter piece being the work of David Mascré, a former member of the Front National politburo. The journal is run by generals from across the armed forces. The fact that it has shown interest in climate change is symptomatic of the reflection currently underway regarding the modalities of collective violence in the decades to come. Of course, military figures' interest in these questions is a way for them to live with the times, in an era in which there is no multinational that does not have a department to deal with ecological questions – including, and perhaps above all those who do most environmental harm (in a phenomenon known as greenwashing). But this interest is also based on deeper-rooted concerns.

In 2012 the French National Assembly devoted a parliamentary report to 'the impact of climate change on defence and security'.[11] This dossier was produced on the initiative of the European Affairs Commission, within the context of debates regarding the emergence of a continent-wide defence policy. Presented by the MPs André Schneider (UMP) and Philippe Tourtelier (PS),[12] the report advanced the hypothesis that in future the army could play the role of a 'chaos specialist'. In this view, the ecological crisis will lead to an aggravation of natural disasters, making the existing institutions – in particular in developing regions – more fragile. In some cases, the army will be the only force capable of intervening to deal with the resulting chaos in an effective manner. Developments of this order are particularly expected in the three zones of strategic interest for the European Union, as identified by this report: the Mediterranean basin, Southwest Asia and the Arctic.

This document examines NATO's intervention after the Pakistan earthquake of 2005. It also takes a look into the role that the Japanese army played in handling the tsunami and nuclear catastrophe at Fukushima in 2011. An event like the 2003 heatwave in continental Europe, which led to some 35,000 deaths, is liable to put health and social security systems under pressure, which opens the way to increased army intervention in handling public health. This parliamentary report was preceded by a 2011 inquiry by the *Centre des hautes études militaires* (CHEM), a training institution for high-ranking officers of the French armed forces.[13] Moreover, the *Délégation aux affaires stratégiques* (DAS), an analysis centre for the French Defence Ministry, created a post for an 'Environment, climate and energy' officer.

The UN Security Council dedicated a session to the climate – as a 'security problem' – in April 2007.[14] China expressed its opposition to such a problem's being addressed in this restricted forum, considering it a question for the international agencies responsible for environmental matters. The UN is also examining the possibility of creating 'green helmets' in order to neutralize conflicts related to climate change. General Secretary Ban Ki-Moon has expressed his support for this initiative.[15]

A benevolent dictatorship

These and many other examples attest to the fact that militaries are taking climate change very seriously indeed. In a moment we shall see why that is the case. The proliferation of military reports concerning this problem and the detail with which it is discussed by the military's organic intellectuals, reveal *a contrario* the difficulties that other segments of the ruling classes have in getting to grips with it. Militaries are today one of the elite sectors – together with finance, as we saw in Chapter 2 – that are capable of reflecting over a thirty to fifty-year horizon, the appropriate temporality for considering the effects of climate change. For its part, the political class is the victim of a 'short-termism' that leaves it ill-able to integrate climate change into its calculations. Indeed, its representatives' near-exclusive objective is to get re-elected at electoral tests that are at most spaced out a few years apart, leaving them little able to take into account more long-term problems.[16]

Militaries, conversely, are accustomed to planning for the medium and long term. Three to five decades is the temporality for strategic analysis – the time that the Cold War took, for example. This is also the average time between a new weapon being conceived and its battlefield deployment. Militaries are also accustomed to handling uncertain situations and this is an integral part of their ethos. As such, they do not find the element of uncertainty inherent in climate change particularly intolerable. As Von Clausewitz says in his *On War*, 'The great uncertainty of all data in War is a peculiar difficulty, because all action must, to a certain extent, be planned in a mere twilight, which in addition not unfrequently – like the effect of a fog or moonshine – gives to things exaggerated dimensions and an unnatural appearance.'[17] Climate change only radicalizes this 'twilight' character of the war environment. Von Clausewitz adds that factors like hydrography, vegetation, relief and temperature play a decisive role in battles' outcome. What is commonly called 'home advantage' refers to the mastery that one of the antagonists has over this set of factors. Armies are 'cognitive' organizations, who amass or produce a volume of data allowing them to bring military actions to a successful conclusion. At this level, they resemble the insurance companies we discussed in Chapter 2. Control of these data is likely to become a very important question, in the context of a changing environment.

Neoliberalism is a modality of capital accumulation in which the financial bourgeoisie has got the upper hand over the other segments of the elite. As Nicos Poulantzas puts it, 'the long term political interest of a power bloc' is organized 'under the bloc hegemony and leadership of one class or fraction' among its components'.[18] Nevertheless, a consequence of crises is to change the balances within the ruling classes. In the long wave of the crisis, different sectors of the elite have a greater or lesser capacity to impose their own interests. Since the end of the Cold War, militaries' power has diminished relative to other factions, in Western countries at least. However, we cannot rule out the possibility that they will regain part of this lost ground thanks to the environmental crisis. Their level of preparation faced with the challenges that this crisis poses and resources they have at hand to deal with it – particularly coercive ones – seem far superior to the ones that other sections of the ruling class have.

The philosopher Hans Jonas, a student of Martin Heidegger and author of *The Imperative of Responsibility* (1979), argues that, in future, humanity will perhaps have to 'accept a halt to its liberty as the necessary price for its physical wellbeing'.[19] Humanity is rushing headlong towards a loss of freedom because it is unable to stop itself inflicting damage on its surroundings. Only a 'benevolent dictatorship' would be capable of taking the measures that are necessary to ensure its 'physical wellbeing'. This is what Jonas calls 'tyranny as an alternative to physical annihilation'.[20] Nothing suggests *a priori* that this will be a *military* tyranny. But the armed forces' degree of preparation faced with the ecological crisis leaves us to suppose that they could well be serious candidates for taking charge. In any event, adaptation to climate change will entail a decisively important military element.

Chaos specialists

What, then, is the link between ecological crisis and the conduct of war, as militaries envisage it? The multiplication of natural disasters implies, first of all, that armies will be increasingly called on to come to the aid of populations – and, in tandem with this, to 'pacify' them. To take two recent examples illustrating this tendency, the 2004 tsunami in the Indian Ocean and 2005's Hurricane Katrina in New Orleans were both very heavily militarized tragedies. The means that were deployed during these operations could not be used for other missions, including in conventional wars. The United States in particular has to deal with this problem, given that it is already engaged in costly wars with uncertain outcomes in Iraq and Afghanistan, not to mention its more indirect involvement in different theatres of operations across all four corners of the world. For the most part, military strategists recognize the state of 'imperial overstretch' that the country finds itself in – to use Paul Kennedy's expression[21] – namely an excessive projection of force considering the means that it has available. Figuring in the background of this assessment is the fiscal crisis in which the USA is now immersed, which we mentioned in the previous chapter. In truth, this crisis affects the majority of industrialized countries. Militaries are not spared the austerity measures to which the crisis has given rise, as the Greek armed forces have recently seen with regard to their budget.[22] Having fallen during the 1990s, worldwide military spending began growing again in the 2000s, even before 11 September 2001. Nonetheless, this tendency seems to have reversed again in recent times, on account of the recession. Moreover, China's emergence as a world power has led Western strategists to predict that significant means will have to be made available, within the context of a new 'containment strategy' whose epicentre may well be the China Sea. One of the most influential international relations theories of the current moment, John Mearsheimer's 'offensive realism', presents an arms race with China as inevitable.[23] In this context, devoting human and material resources to humanitarian operations resulting from the ecological crisis risks making the armed forces' job rather more complicated.

One expression frequently repeated in militaries' thinking on the ecological crisis is 'threat multiplier'. Climate change will not necessarily create new threats. Nonetheless, it will aggravate problems that already exist, in particular in regions at risk – notably Africa, Asia and Latin America. Inequalities, corruption and 'inter-ethnic' conflicts will increase on account of resources becoming rarer or disasters more frequent. The Darfur case mentioned in Chapter 1, which often reappears in this literature, is presented as typical of the lethal interaction of ethnicity, climate and war. Global warming will, moreover, encourage certain illnesses like malaria, dengue fever or salmonella poisoning to spread beyond their ecosystem, thus increasing the pressure on healthcare systems.[24]

The 'multiplication of threats' will especially affect water. Most of the great rivers of Asia – the Indus, Ganges, Yangtzee, the Mekong . . . – have their source in the Himalayas. Melting glaciers, coupled with the construction of hydroelectric dams, threaten to lead to major water shortages in this region.[25] Moreover, this problem is also taking on a geopolitical dimension. The Himalayan glaciers feeding these Asian rivers are for the most part to be found in Chinese territory. The tensions between China and its neighbours in relation to the sharing of water reserves promises to increase, as is already the case between China and India, particularly over China's plan to divert the Brahmaputra river.[26] Shortages will accelerate the rhythm of urbanization in the surrounding countries. In making irrigation more uncertain and thus rendering agriculture less productive, they will encourage peasants to abandon their land and move to the 'planet of slums' proliferating around the planet's great urban centres.[27] Guerrillas – but also violence linked to narcotrafficking – are ever more centred on this planet of slums, and no longer in the rural space like in Mao and Che Guevara's day. The urbanization of war is a phenomenon that a number of contemporary

theorists of war have highlighted.[28] The climate crisis is one
of the factors contributing to this.

Terrorism and climate change

In militaries' eyes, climate change risks undermining certain
states that are already weak and strategically sensitive. These
are the famous 'failed states' as theorized by the Pentagon
since the George H. W. Bush and Bill Clinton administrations.
Failed states are those considered incapable of providing the
'normal' functions of a modern democratic state: security,
justice, equality before the law . . . For the most part they are
situated in what used to be called the Third World. Each year
Foreign Policy, the review founded by Samuel Huntington,
publishes a ranking of these states called the *Failed States
Index*.[29] There are around fifty of these states, though it is a
list that develops from year to year. In 2010, Somalia was the
world's most failed state, followed by Chad and Sudan. The
top rankings remained unchanged in 2011. Haiti was the
most failed non-African state and Afghanistan the most failed
Asian one.

This ranking is established on the basis of a dozen criteria.
Every country gets a score on each of these points, ranging
from 'demographic pressure' to the existence of 'public services', via 'government legitimacy' and 'economic development'. Iraq occupied the top places in this ranking until the
mid 2000s, but since then has fallen to ninth place, seemingly
on account of the Americans' effective nation-building. Each
year the *Failed States Index* is illustrated with a series of
photographs entitled *Postcards from hell*.[30] These display
some of the situations of poverty and hopelessness located in
failed states: Liberia, Bangladesh, North Korea, Kyrgyzstan
. . . From the mother crying for the loss of her landslide-
victim children to the line of soldiers blocking a famished
crowd's path, passing by way of devout Muslims kneeled in
prayer, the world painted by these photos – each of them
accompanied by a catastrophist-inflected caption – is that of
an inevitable and naturalized barbarism.

One hypothesis advanced by numerous geostrategists since
the end of the Cold War holds that the breeding ground for

twenty-first century conflicts will be weak states and, in particular, 'failed states'. Robert Kaplan notably advanced this
argument in an influential article for *The Atlantic* magazine
entitled 'The coming anarchy'.[31] The anarchy evoked in the
title will be the result of the break-up of the balances of the
Cold War era. The vectors of the conflicts of the twentieth
century were strong states. This was true of both the two
World Wars, in which the main world powers clashed, and
the Cold War. During this latter conflict there were numerous
proxy wars among weak nations, in particular in the Third
World. But they were overdetermined by superpower relations. Today peace reigns among strong states, even if they
do directly or indirectly cause plenty of conflicts in the rest
of the world. War has been displaced to weak states. They
are even less able to do so as the climate crisis denies both
the means and stability they need.

The conclusion of this line of argument is a simple one.
Militaries' concern over climate change is closely linked to
the dominant strategic paradigm of the post Cold War period:
the struggle against 'terrorism'. Their reading of climate
change is overdetermined by an obsession that they had even
before 11 September 2001 and which this event further inten-
sified. For the armed forces, terrorism and climate change first
of all have in common the fact that they are both transnational phenomena that no one state can fight alone. That is
why this phenomenon may well help rejuvenate international
organizations like NATO. But there is also a second link
between terrorism and ecological crisis, in that this crisis
provides a breeding ground for terrorism to prosper, especially in 'failed states'. Climate change and (the struggle
against) terrorism are, therefore, two phenomena that militaries consider in combination with one another.

The new military ecology

The end of the Cold War gave rise to what Noam Chomsky
has called a 'new military humanism'.[32] This expression refers
to the imperialist expeditions that Western states have waged
since the 1980s in the guise of promoting democracy and
human rights. We have seen this from Iraq to Kosovo, Bosnia,

Somalia, Sudan, Afghanistan and, more recently, in Libya. This new humanism is military because it is based on aerial bombing campaigns, often accompanied by troops putting 'boots on the ground'. Nonetheless, it includes an important civilian component. Wherever they intervene, Western armed forces set up 'non-combatant' operations to improve the well-being of the populations concerned. The goal, here, is to crush potential conflicts in the egg, to make trafficking and piracy less attractive options and even to secure local collaboration in the struggle against uprisings.

Part of this new military humanism consists of a new military *ecology*. The US armed forces command in Africa – AFRICOM – has chartered numerous naval ships in the region in an operation called 'Africa Partnership Station'.[33] George Bush's Defense Secretary Donald Rumsfeld was among the instigators of this initiative. It first emerged as an extension of the help that the US Navy brought to the countries that fell victim to the 2004 Indian Ocean tsunami. The US armed forces' two principal concerns in Africa are terrorism and oil. The 1998 attacks on the country's embassies in Kenya and Tanzania caused more than two hundred deaths. Since then, movements hostile to US interests have proliferated on the African continent, some of them in connection to transnational networks. Moreover, today more than 15 per cent of US oil comes from Africa. By 2020 this figure could hit 25 or even 40 per cent.

The Africa Partnership Station is engaged in traditional military operations. Nonetheless, its mission also consists of training local armies and police forces, protecting fish stocks, ensuring the circulation of metal ores and oil and maintaining water and forest resources – and all this in collaboration with the states and populations of the region. Particularly in West Africa, illegal fishing has disastrous consequences for the oceans and for the populations who live off fishing resources. One British NGO counted 252 cases of illegal fishing between January 2010 and July 2012 in Sierra Leone's territorial waters alone.[34] This new military humanism has a long history. Even in 1966, under Lyndon B. Johnson's presidency, an American fleet delivered seeds and food aid to India during a famine. The slogan widely used at the time was 'Feed'em or fight'em'; famines in Third World countries could give rise to revolutions hostile to US interests, so it was preferable to pre-empt such upheavals by feeding the populations concerned.[35]

One technical mechanism recently put in place in order to help these missions run smoothly is called 'seabasing'.[36] As its name suggests, this consists of using the sea as a base, in order to rely as little as possible on land-based infrastructure. After all, bases on land are at the mercy of insurgents, as the US Army has seen even recently in Iraq and Afghanistan. Remaining at sea offers a shelter from attacks. It also makes it easier not to appear before the population concerned as an occupying force. Operations following the 2010 earthquake in Haiti, bringing aid and seeking to maintain order, were an opportunity to try out this mechanism on a large scale. The disaster had destroyed the country's ports and its airports were quickly overburdened. Projecting the armed forces' power from seabases made it possible to get around such obstacles.

Rising sea levels threaten to cause great damage to numerous countries' coastal and delta areas. There is the risk that this will hamper troops disembarking and moving onto land. The solution? Seabasing, which allows the armed forces effectively to intervene in crisis situations, while sparing the logistical constraints that result from a more and more unpredictable 'operational environment'. As we see, climate change brings innovation also in the domains of military tactics and logistics.

The new military ecology is currently being applied in Afghanistan. Not only militaries *stricto sensu* are doing battle in this country. National or international organizations like USAID or the UN environment programme are playing a decisive role in putting the country back on its feet. In 2005, the 'Green Afghanistan Initiative' – whose participants include many international organizations, including UNICEF and the FAO, as well as Afghan ministers – undertook to a 'post-conflict environmental evaluation'.[37] It noted that Afghanistan's nature has considerably suffered from the war, in particular on account of the conflict's effect on biodiversity. The country has also suffered from the unregulated use of pastureland, uncontrolled deforestation and an ever-more deprived population's over-use of water resources.

A programme for protecting the environment was thus agreed, with its measures including reforestation, the regeneration of the soil, the establishment of an appropriate legal framework, as well as 'changing attitudes towards the environment'. Moreover, this initiative encourages 'micro-enterprise' in agricultural production and the privatization of communal lands. The underlying hypothesis today hegemonic among the international organizations working in this field of development holds that the 'empowerment' of individuals is the best way to secure results in preserving the environment.

In Afghanistan, there is an interaction between climate crisis and Taliban insurgency, as mediated by drug trafficking. The persistence of the opium trade in this country is partly explained by the fact that poppy-growing does not take much water, consuming only a sixth of the amount needed to grow wheat. For this reason, poppies are more resistant to droughts than other crops are. The province that produces the greatest quantities of opium, Kargahar, is also one of those most subject to drought.[38] The multiplication and intensification of climate phenomena make it improbable that these populations will turn to other types of crops in future (and, indeed, the opium trade represents more than a third of Afghanistan's GDP). The Taliban tolerate this trade, which helps explain the support that they enjoy among wide layers of the population. Moreover, the Taliban are often themselves peasants who passed through refugee camps and madrassas after falling victim to droughts or flooding.[39] In turn, the money that comes from growing poppies allows the Taliban to get hold of weapons and to strengthen their positions. Recognizing this fact, one US military report states that re-establishing 'natural security' is a prime strategic objective for the NATO armies in Afghanistan.[40] Offering realistic alternatives to opium by increasing agricultural productivity would make it possible to break the causal chain linking climate, opium and armed insurgency.

Conservation and counter-insurgency

Counter-insurgency doctrines have always included an environmental element. A recent French army manual entitled

Principes de contre-insurrection, put together by the colonels Hervé de Courrèges, Emmanuel Germain and Nicolas Le Nen, tracks the history of counter-insurgency from Little Big Horn in 1876 to the Taliban, via Vietnam and Mogadishu. Medical metaphors are widespread in the military sphere and, in particular, in the domain of counter-insurgency. Discussing the 'territorial marginalization' of insurgencies, the authors declare that 'After an antiseptic phase that wipes clean the wound and its edges, the process continues with the application of a fine-mesh sterile gauze, keeping the now cleaned-up area sanitized.'[41]

Guerrilla wars are characterized by insurgents 'melting into' with the local population. Counter-insurgency's objective is to isolate the former from the latter, in order to 'treat' this problem effectively. It has a panoply of possible measures at hand in order to achieve this. One of these is the improvement of the population's wellbeing, which will supposedly encourage it to break with the insurgents and collaborate with the counter-insurgency operation. The 'Briggs Plan' that the British enacted in Malaysia in the 1950s, which displaced more than half a million Malaysians of Chinese origin towards 'new villages' or 'strategic hamlets', was one example of this approach. 'The objective', the French colonels explain, 'was to make life in the new villages easier and more attractive than in the old, illegal ones.'[42] This plan was one of the first in history implementing a so-called 'hearts and minds' strategy, where the counter-insurgency does not only mount a 'search and destroy' strategy to eradicate the insurgents, but also seeks to win the favour of the local population. It emphasized improving living conditions: roads, schools, but also irrigation systems and new arable land. Also expressing this same approach was the US Army's *Counter-insurgency Field Manual 3–24*, issued in 2006 in response to the failure of counter-insurgency in Iraq and Afghanistan. This document appeared under the name of General David Petraeus, at that time commander of the Western forces in Afghanistan.

Few armies anywhere in the world have the same experience of counter-insurgency as does the Indian army. And there is a reason for this: guerrillas have been operating in this country ever since its independence. The best-known guerrilla force is the Naxalites, who take their name from the village of Naxalbari, situated in West Bengal, in the east of India. This rebellion – some sections of which are of Maoist inspiration – first emerged in the 1960s, with the overexploitation of the forests providing its breeding ground. The industrialization of India is partly based on extractive industries: the exploitation of metal ores, wood, coal and land.[43] The appropriation of these resources is the object of a struggle among the federal state, foreign multinations and local populations, including the Adivasi (Hindi for 'first inhabitants'). The energy needs that this development requires gives rise to the construction of large dams, leading to massive population displacements. India today counts thirty to forty million displaced people. The popular support for the Naxalites can only be understood in this context. The population is the victim of a large-scale process of 'accumulation by dispossession' – to use David Harvey's term.[44] In 2009, the army launched an operation in the 'red corridor' in the east of the country, entitled 'Operation Green Hunt', aimed at eradicating the Naxalites. India is also home to 'the world's highest battlefield', the Siachen glacier. Situated at the crossroads of India, China and Pakistan on the Karakoram mountain range (to the north of Kashmir) – often called the 'third pole' because of its size – this glacier has for thirty years been the theatre of a clash between the Indian and Pakistani armies. Contrary to the worldwide tendency, the glaciers of this range have not retreated in recent decades – but the exception is Siachen, which is rapidly melting away. One of the causes of this is military activity.[45] On the Indian side alone, more than a tonne of waste is thrown into the glacier's crevices each year. Biodiversity and hydrology suffer from the presence of the troops. The transportation of materiel and soldiers involves a significant amount of fossil fuel consumption. Daily helicopter flights, the pipelines channelling oil in order to heat the igloos inhabited by the soldiers, as well as the kerosene stoves used to keep their weapons warm, are so many factors contributing to the degradation of this environment. All this has led the Indian army to develop a genuine *savoir-faire* of military ecology. That is what emerges from the writings of P. K. Gautam, an Indian theorist of 'natural security'. Gautam is a retired colonel and a researcher at the Institute for Defense Studies and Analysis.[46] At one time he was an officer based at the Siachen glacier, perhaps explaining his interest in these questions. The Indian army, Gautam says, was the first in the world to establish 'ecological task forces'.[47] The idea goes back to the early 1980s and the prime minister of the time, Indira Gandhi. These dozen task force units go around the country working on nature preservation projects: reforesting, stabilizing sand dunes, preserving pastureland and soil, purifying water . . . The backdrop to this is the idea that preserving nature contributes to peace and the sta-blility of the social order. China's People's Liberation Army (PLA) also takes on this type of tasks. Purporting to be an emanation of a revolutionary people, the PLA has a long-standing tradition of humanitarian intervention in the event of disasters.[48]

Econationalism

One of these ecological task forces' objectives is to protect 'the nation's biodiversity'.[49] According to P. K. Gautam, this biodiversity is part of Indian identity itself, since over the ages this latter has formed through contact with the subcontinent's luxuriant nature. In this sense, preserving 'the nation's biodiversity' and defending national identity is one and the same thing. On this point, Gautam remarks that a large proportion of Indian soldiers come from peasant families and thus have a 'spontaneous' understanding of the environment – indigenous knowledges and *savoir-faire* that have been accumulated from generation to generation. He adds that the army should be doing more to profit from these knowledges and *savoir-faire*, within the context of its nature-protection activities.

In his theory of nationalism, Benedict Anderson demonstrates that if nationalism is to prosper it has to become incarnated in concrete institutions.[50] He turns his gaze to three of them, namely cartography, which delimits the borders of the national territory; the census, an inventory of the nation's members; and museums, which give it its collective memory. Nature, too, is one of the institutions that contribute to the construction of national identity in the modern age. There is an ecological nationalism – an econationalism – distinguished by the link that it establishes between a nation's mindset and the environment in which it operates. As we have seen, in the United States, the supposedly unspoilt great natural spaces that the Americans have since the nineteenth century called 'wilderness' are one of the nation's founding myths.[51] A 2007 Sean Penn film entitled *Into the Wild* recently reminded us of this. As the Indian radical historian Ramachandra Guha explains, natural parks – for example Yellowstone and Yosemite, which are two of the oldest ones – are considered a contribution to human civilization that specifically owes to the United States.[52] It goes without saying that the spaces in question have never been 'untouched'; rather, they were cleared of their Native American populations. Moreover, if they are 'natural' this does not mean that they are accessible to all Americans without distinction of class or race.

We also see this econationalism in the Middle East. In the twentieth century the rising power of Arab nationalism went hand-in-hand with the question of oil. For example, Iraq's Ba'ath Party advanced the slogan 'Arab oil to the Arabs', as the basis for the nationalizations of the early 1970s.[53] The income coming from oil extraction long served to finance development and restribution policies. For his part, Muammar Gaddafi said that oil was the 'fuel of the revolution', both in Libya and on a pan-African scale. 'Taking control of the oil sector was felt to be historic revenge . . . [The foreign oil companies'] control over energy resources stopped these regimes and the fierce nationalism and socialist ideology of pan-Arabism from turning the page on the colonial past'.[54] Turning the page would first require expropriating these companies and handing the oil over to its rightful owners: the peoples of the region. Nationalism, anti-imperialism and natural resources are thus inextricably mixed together.

Initiatives similar to India's ecological task forces also exist in other countries. Since the late 1970s the UK Defence Ministry has organized 'conservation groups'. It periodically gives these groups access to its military bases, so that they can observe the wildlife to be found there. This initiative is a response to the anti-militarism of the 1960s and 1970s, one of whose criticisms of the armed forces was the damage that they cause to nature in the areas they control. In France, the struggle against the expansion of the Larzac base in the early

1970s was also based on this critique. Certain armed forces tackle the problem head-on, which gives rise to a 'military environmentalism' or 'khaki conservation'.[55] They argue that flora and fauna are best protected in military areas; after all, activities that endanger biodiversity such as tourism, agriculture and urbanization do not take place therein. Of course, such a claim should be subject to caution, to say the least.[56] Yet we can sometimes see the most amazing phenomena; for example, it has been demonstrated that the military zone separating the two Koreas is home to many dozens of rare species.[57]

Agent Orange

However, counter-insurgency is more classically based on the destruction of the environment than on its conservation. In actual fact, the dialectic of conservation and destruction is at the heart of the military construction of nature. This is evident in the case of the Vietnam War. Faced with the powerful US armed forces, the Vietcong – the 'South Vietnam National Liberation Front' – faced a very unfavourable balance of forces. Like a number of guerrillas since the beginning of the modern age, it used nature tactically – in this case, the jungle that covers large swathes of the country. This allowed it to create surprise effects or to take shelter when it was retreating. In cases of asymmetrical warfare, forest is a 'force equalizer'.[58]

In order to take back the advantage, the US military used herbicides, including the well-known Agent Orange. The objective was a simple one: to gain increased visibility in Vietnam's thick jungle and thus to destroy the guerrilla ecosystem. We might mention in passing that Agent Orange was a creation of the multinational Monsanto, which today specializes in GM production. As such, in the Ranch Hand operation running between 1962 and 1971, tens of thousands of cubic metres of defoliants were poured over the country, exposing[59] 3.3 million hectares of vegetation to these herbicides. 22,000 km^2 of forests were defoliated, more than 20 per cent of the country's forest regions. A World Bank report concludes that the war changed Vietnam's biodiversity in a lasting manner. Agent Orange also contaminated the food chain. One study shows that the pollution of the soil has passed on to animals and that traces of certain among its toxic components are found in human milk and human blood.[60]

Of course, the Vietnam War was not the first where the destruction of ecosystems was used as a military tactic. For example, the French used firebombs to destroy vegetation in the Rif War of 1921 to 1926, as did the Americans in 1946 to 1949 in the areas occupied by the communist resistance during the Greek Civil War.[61]

War has long made use of forests. Wood provided a material for making primitive weapons like bows, arrows and spears. The appearance of metallic weapons of bronze and iron five thousand years ago was not the end to wood's role as an essential element of armaments. Wagons transporting soldiers and materiel, as well as boats and fortifications, were also made of wood. Up until the nineteenth century no imperialism and no political power was conceivable without mastery over the wood supply. In a different field, from the Middle Ages onward the construction of cathedrals and churches – material bases of the dominant Christian ideology – required colossal volumes of wood.[62] It was the nations that could avail themselves of a certain 'ecological profile'[63] – the ones that controlled the forests – that became imperialist. Such was the case for the nations that became Atlantic powers after the discovery of the Americas. Cuba and the Philippines were colonies fundamental to the Spanish Empire, not only because they had an economic interest in themselves, but because the forests situated there fed the colonial enterprise in general. The same goes, in the French and British cases, for the forests of North America.

The threshold of the modern age, around the seventeenth century, saw what historians usually call the 'military revolution'.[64] Among other factors, this was the fruit of the generalization of the use of gunpowder, the increase in military budgets and the number of soldiers and the rationalization of military organization. The backdrop to this was the emergence of nation-states and modern peoples. With more numerous and powerful armed forces, the demand for wood increased yet further, since all military infrastructure (barracks, weapons, transport) was dependent on it. Only in the second half of the nineteenth century did this demand begin to decline. The appearance of a new combustible, coal, also in part explains this decline. The First Opium War, which the Britain Empire fought in China between 1839 and 1842, heralded the alliance of war and coal.[65] The transition from wood to coal, from coal to oil, and then from oil to nuclear, transformed the manner in which war is waged. Each of these transitions was a partial one, with each rising resource over-lapping – for a time, at least – with the preceding one. And each of them makes new tactics possible. The German *Blitz-krieg* in the Second World War would have been inconceiv-able without the motor power provided by petrol.[66]

Forests are also part of the very configuration of the battle-field, as we saw in the Vietnamese example. They permit or impede the movement of cavalry and infantry, be it motor-ized or otherwise. Clausewitz recommended never retreating through forest, in order to avoid having to fight 'blindly', without knowing the enemy's progress and its positions.[67] The age-old practice of 'scorched earth' is another modality of the military construction of nature. This practice goes back (at least) to the war between the Persians and the Scythians of 512 BCE, when these latter set fire to their own lands in order to impede the Persians' advance.[68] The 'trench warfare' or 'war of position' organized during the First World War also had environmental implications. The forests of Verdun were affected in lasting fashion by the battle that raged there during the Great War.[69]

From the Cold War to green wars

Militaries' interest in environmental questions ought to be set within a long-term strategic context, with the end of the Cold War and its characteristic political–military theories (strategy of containment, nuclear deterrents, the domino-effect theory . . .) The idea of green wars is inscribed in powerful tenden-cies in the modalities of collective violence. More precisely, in the paradigm of 'new wars'. This expression refers to the developments in the art of war since the last third of the twentieth century and in particular since the fall of the Berlin

Wall. These developments are, of course, inscribed in long and discordant temporalities, but it is in recent decades that they have crystallized.[70]

What are the 'new wars'? With the new wars, the distinction between combatants and non-combatants, soldiers and civilians, tends to be blurred. From the Napoleonic Wars up to the two World Wars, this distinction was always very much a relative one. Nonetheless, it was a structuring principle of modern armed conflicts, on both the juridical and strategic planes. Two elements of the Second World War – bombing from the air and German occupation – would accelerate the erosion of this principle.[71] Bombs dropped from the skies made no distinction between soldiers and civilians, while the resistance to occupation was waged by civilians who became soldiers (or vice versa). Before the Second World War, aerial bombings and military occupation had already been experienced in the colonial context;[72] and in this sense the true origin of the new wars is doubtless found in colonial wars. At the beginning of the twentieth century, 90 per cent of the victims of war were soldiers. In the Second World War, this percentage reached 50–50. By the end of the 1990s, 80 per cent of the victims were civilians.[73]

With the weakening of the distinction between combatants and non-combatants, the delimitation between the front line and the rear also disappeared. 'New wars' stand apart from the 'war of position' characteristic of the First World War, which supposes the existence of stable front lines. In principle, modern wars among states play out in a specific space-time, separate from the rest of the social world; on the battlefield and, more often than not, by day. This space-time remains open between the moment when the belligerents declare war and the moment that they sign an armistice. The new wars set this spatial–temporal mechanism in crisis. Some have gone so far as to say that the distinction between war and peace is today obsolete, now having been replaced with permanent 'states of violence'.[74] The new wars are wars of movement, where the front and the rear, as well as lines of communication and logistics, are constantly evolving. Guerrilla wars – the wars of movement *par excellence* – are another matrix of the new wars. Today we are also seeing siege warfare coming back into force – the warfare typical of medieval wars, of which there were many examples in the conflict in former Yugoslavia, including, among others, the sieges of Sarajevo and Dubrovnik.

The new wars also entail an 'identitarian' dimension.[75] Since the French Revolution, wars have always been linked to national sentiments, in one way or another. They also contribute to the construction of such feeling, by way of conscription or through the designation of the nation's enemies. The new wars are part of the crisis and reconfiguration of contemporary nation-states. They often result from the disaggregation 'from below' of pre-existing political entities, as in the cases of Yugoslavia and the USSR, or from certain states' incapacity to conserve a monopoly of legitimate violence. Infra- or proto-national identities are frequently vectors of the new wars. This is what explains the new wars' tendency to give rise to forms of 'ethnic cleansing'.

The end of conventional wars?

Not only regular forces are engaged in the new wars. Paramilitary groups, foreign mercenaries, self-defence units and regular foreign troops – sometimes under UN mandate – enter into the mix, together with the armed forces of the belligerent countries.[76] The privatization of war is a phenomenon recorded by a number of strategists. With the 'military revolution' mentioned above, war (mainly) became a matter of states, in the sense that it was waged by powerful bureaucracies. As Nicos Poulantzas puts it, 'unlike its pre-capitalist counterparts, this supremely juridical State holds a monopoly of violence and ultimate terror, *a monopoly of war*'.[77] Yet now we are seeing mercenaries coming back into force.[78] In 2010, this industry amounted to $200bn at the global scale, employing one million people. In 2011 there were more mercenaries contracted by the Pentagon in Iraq and Afghanistan than there were regular forces; 145,000 in the former case, 155,000 in the latter.[79] Neoliberalism is no stranger to this tendency. The dynamic of subcontracting characteristic of neoliberalism leads large enterprises to delegate part of their activity in order to reduce their costs. The same goes for the military domain and we can add to this the fact that after the

Cold War armed forces saw their budgets and personnel numbers reduced. A number of soldiers found themselves unemployed and so they were prepared to accept employment in 'security' companies. This partly explains the fragmentation of states' monopoly over the legitimate use of violence in the contemporary period.

We can count on the fingers of our hands the 'conventional' conflicts between states that have taken place since the Second World War. The examples that come to mind are the wars between India and Pakistan; between Israel and the Arab states (up until the 1973 Yom Kippur conflict); between Iran and Iraq; between Greece and Turkey; etc. Most conflicts since 1945 have been 'low-intensity' wars, in the sense that they do not, as such, set state against state. This is often explained on account of the existence of the atomic bomb. Theorists of nuclear deterrence maintain that nuclear weaponry has had a pacifying effect on international relations, rendering war potentially so disastrous that it has forced the nations who possess such weaponry to show restraint.[80] As Thomas Schelling said in his 2005 Nobel Prize for Economics acceptance speech, 'the most spectacular event of the past half century is one that did not occur'.[81] The argument that the bomb has had a pacifying effect is, however, a manifestly false one, since collective violence has not in fact diminished in either quantity or intensity since the end of the Second World War. Yet it has changed in scale, with collective violence now being deployed more on an infra-state level.[82]

Given this set of factors, one of the deftest theorists of the new wars, Martin Van Creveld, has concluded that modern war – which he calls 'Clausewitzian war' – is on the point of disappearing. Clausewitzian war emerged with the 1648 Treaty of Westphalia. It is based on the principle of national sovereignty and the codification of the relations among nations in international law, including the laws of war. This is a political order in the strong sense: states' behaviour and in particular the decision to declare war are governed by a calculation of power relations. That is the reason why Clausewitz could say, a little short of two centuries later, that war is the continuation of politics by other means. In this perspective, armed conflict is subordinate to states' political objectives. According to Van Creveld, Clausewitzian war is today being replaced by a 'war for existence'. Here, war is no longer the continuation of politics by other means; it stops being Clausewitzian. War is no longer principally waged by states, and the element of 'irrationality' involved tends to increase.

Double movement

We could criticize many aspects of 'new wars' theory. For example, it gives a very poor account of the 'new imperialism' that appeared after the fall of the USSR – that is to say, the West's imperialist exploits over the course of the last three decades. Be that as it may, the important thing is that the 'new wars' and green wars are closely linked. The 'new wars' often involve an environmental dimension, to the point that some have even spoken of a 'political ecology of war'.[83] Shortages of resources – of water, arable land, fish stocks or pasturelands – and the degradation of ecosystems more generally have contributed to the emergence of armed conflicts of this type.[84] The causal link is never a unilateral one, and natural factors always come to interact with other ones: demographic pressure, the availability of weaponry, interference by foreign powers, social inequalities, forms of ethno-racial discrimination . . . But the 'war for existence' to which Van Creveld refers simultaneously both stems from and generates the increasing scarcity of resources and the destruction of ecosystems.

The Israeli–Palestinian conflict provides a textbook case of a political ecology of war. It is estimated that the annual production of drinkable water in Israel amounts to 1.95 million cubic metres.[85] The State of Israel's water requirements, including those of the settlers in the occupied territories, are 10 per cent greater than this figure. The difference is made up by the over-exploitation of aquifers – underground layers containing water tables. This over-exploitation can eventually leave the wells running dry. Two of the three aquifers on which Israel's water supply depends sit under West Bank territory. And of course, an Arab's and an Israeli's access to water resources is not the same. The Israeli settlers consume four times more water than the Arabs.[86] The Israeli army strictly limits the Arabs' access to water. The consequences of this include, among other things, a number of Palestinian farmers being forced to abandon their land and move to the towns.

Of course, we could never reduce such a long and complex conflict to a question of the water supply alone. But it is one of the factors that feed conflict and, given the climate crisis, it is unlikely that this situation is going to improve in the years to come. Indeed, it is estimated that by 2020, 75 to 250 million people in Africa will have difficulties accessing drinkable water.

A similar type of process also partly explains the situation of collective violence – though not a war – in South Africa. This country has one of the world's highest crime rates. In the 1980s Apartheid led to hundreds of thousands of poor Blacks being clustered together on the country's least productive land, with the lowest supply of natural resources.[87] Here we see how the political ecology of war interacts with racial factors, as we observed in Chapter 1. Hence, in the Ciskei Bantustan in Cape Province, the population density reached 82 inhabitants per km^2, whereas it stood at just two inhabitants per km^2 for the rest of the province. The woods were rapidly transformed into combustible fuel for heating, the pasturelands were over-exploited and arable land was eroded. As such, the local ecology, combined with the state's repressive activity, provided no kind of basis for long-term development. The consequence, once Apartheid was abolished, was a rural exodus and the arrival of internal migrants in towns little able to offer them employment. This goes to explain one of the causes of South Africa's high crime rate today.

We could provide countless examples of this problem, which can be summarized as follows: 'Falling agricultural production, migration to urban areas and economic contraction in regions severely affected by scarcity often produce hardship and this hardship increases demands on the state. At the same time, scarcity can interfere with state revenue streams by reducing economic productivity and therefore taxes . . . Environmental scarcity therefore increases society's demands on the state while decreasing [the state's] ability to meet those demands.'[88]

Collective violence follows from a 'double movement', to use an expression employed by Karl Polanyi in another

context.[89] On the one hand, resource shortages and the multiplication of natural disasters place strains on agricultural
production, driving increased poverty and thus placing greater
demands on the state. On the other hand, this strain decreases
the means that the state has at hand, since it decreases tax
revenues and thus the state's capacity to intervene in an effective way. The greater the share of the relevant country's GDP
is represented by the agricultural sector, the more it will be
affected by this double movement. And the crisis is all the
more devastating when the state that has to deal with it is
already a fragile one. So we see a sort of spatial–temporal
circulation of the crisis: the environmental crisis transforms
into a crisis of agriculture, which gives rise to a rural exodus,
thus increasing the pressure on public services and the labour
market in the urban context. This is a process liable – given
certain conditions – to encourage collective violence.

However, the causal chain may also proceed in the opposite direction, from towns to countryside.[90] The shortage of
natural resources is sometimes the result of pillage and piracy.
Underpinning the planet of slums is an underground economy
with an exchange of livestock, wood, fish and metal ores
arriving from the countryside. This underground economy is
itself sustained by the 'above-ground' economy's inability to
provide populations with means of subsistence. In this sense,
the urban crisis tends to feed shortages and poverty in the
rural context. Moreover, collective violence can arise not only
because of resource shortages, but even due to their abundance. In such cases, the conflict is fought over the appropriation of the resources concerned. Precious stones and oil are
classic cases of goods whose presence on a territory has given
rise to wars, for example in Africa. Since the postwar period
political scientists have widely discussed the question of the
'resource curse':[91] to what degree does a country's possession
of resources fuel its greedier impulses and does it give rise to
war? If a resource eventually becomes a country's only source
of revenue, does it impede its development?

Moreover, the populations of developing countries devote
a greater proportion of their incomes to food – of the order
of 35 per cent – than do the populations of developed countries, where this figure falls to 10 per cent. This implies that
variations in the price of foodstuffs on the world market, for

example on account of droughts, have a relatively greater impact on their purchasing power. Indeed, the nine biggest wheat importers are all in the Middle East, which is not a region conducive to growing this crop. Seven of these nine were outposts of the 'Arab Spring'.[92] Among other factors, we could hypothesize an indirect – but real – causal relation between the increase in the prices of certain foodstuffs following droughts in the producer countries in the second half of the 2000s and these popular revolts.

'Hunger riots' frequently recur throughout the history of modern revolutions. We might recall that many of the demonstrators in Tunisia and Egypt, for example, were brandishing loaves of bread. In the sociology of the revolutions of the twenty-first century, there is a good chance that pressure on food prices will figure prominently among the explanatory factors.

Climate refugees

One effect of the ecological crisis is that it creates 'climate refugees'. A climate refugee is a person whose decision to migrate is wholly or partly linked to environmental factors. These refugees are sometimes presented as the 'missing link' that attaches economic crisis to the political tensions that may ultimately result: the crisis produces refugees and their migratory movements destabilize the regions where they arrive.[93] For example, this can give rise to 'inter-ethnic' conflicts. In this sense, ecological crisis and political crisis are mediated by climate-driven migration patterns.

The number of climate refugees in the world today is estimated at 25 million.[94] Predictions for the future situation differ, but certain analysts foresee between 50 and 200 million refugees of this kind by 2050. There have always been migration movements linked to climate. The 'Dust Bowl' that John Steinbeck portrays in *The Grapes of Wrath* is one well-known example of this phenomenon. In the 1930s, during the Great Depression, the southwest USA – and especially Oklahoma and Texas – fell victim to dust storms. The combination of recurrent droughts and intensive agriculture made the land unproductive. This gave rise to migration by the

'Okies' – the farmers who lived in Oklahoma (and the surrounding states) – many of whom now became agricultural labourers in California. Hurricane Katrina is a latter-day 'Dust Bowl', even if one with different modalities.

The notion of 'climate refugees' is the object of controversies among both international organizations and migration specialists. Three problematics structure this debate. First of all, determinism. An individual's decision to migrate is the fruit of a complex set of causal factors. As such, it would be analytically erroneous and politically dangerous to look to any 'climate determinism' to explain the choice to migrate. Moreover, to this day the UN High Commissioner for Refugees (UNHCR) does not recognize the category 'climate refugee', even though it does provide assistance to the victims of natural disasters, such as the 2004 tsunami in the Indian Ocean.[95] As the argument goes, an ill-considered extension of the category 'refugee' would risk endangering those who really are refugees, from the standpoint of international law and in particular 'political' refugees. Other international organizations have, however, adopted and promoted the use of this category. One of the first references to 'climate refugees' appeared in a UN Environment Programme report dating back to 1985. The Intergovernmental Panel on Climate Change also mentions this problematic in its 2007 report. The 'Stern Report' submitted to the UK government in 2006 also devoted attention to climate refugees. This report – which takes its name from Nicholas Stern, an economist specializing in 'sustainable development' – is, for mainstream ecology, an authoritative source on everything to do with the economy and quantifying climate change.

A third aspect of the question: should we speak of climate 'refugees' or climate 'migrants'?[96] This is a major difference. In the first case, the individual concerned is considered to have been forced to migrate. In the second case, it is a matter of personal choice. When this notion first appeared, the category 'refugee' was widely used, but since the 1990s a tendency has emerged for the term 'migrant' to become more and more frequently used instead. In this change, we can see the growing power of a neoliberal approach to handling the climate crisis. 'Migrants' instead tend to be perceived as 'entrepreneurs' able to master their own destiny; in this perspective, migration is one of several possibilities that lay open to them.

Several factors are contributing to the appearance of climate refugees: natural disasters, rising sea levels and the increasing scarcity of water resources.[97] Given that more than two-thirds of the world's population live within 100 km of the coast, rising sea levels will significantly affect migration.[98] Migrants often move near to the coast, since that is where economic opportunities most often arise. Most climate migration, like migration in general, is internal to the departure country and not international in character. For example, the droughts and flooding hitting the northeast of Brazil have encouraged the population of this region to migrate to the country's big cities.[99] This is particularly feeding the growth of the *favelas* of Rio and São Paolo. Combined with other factors, such internal climate migration fuels the poverty and violence raging in these areas. Firearms claim twenty to thirty thousand lives in Brazil each year. Here again, the crisis passes through a series of different states: a climate crisis transforms into an economic, social and political one – and vice versa.

The authors of the French parliament report – mentioned above – devoted to the consequences that climate change has for 'security', warn of the danger that climate refugees represent. For the purposes of protecting Europe from this danger, they recommend the establishment of 'strengthened naval protection' in the Mediterranean in order to handle migration flows, providing the European coastguards with a real warrant for action.[100]

In the same order of thinking, India has built a 4,000 km wall along its border with Bangladesh.[101] The argument used to justify this wall – the longest one in the world separating two countries – is protection against terrorism, drug trafficking and migration flows. The persistent floods of which Bangladesh is the victim, and thus the loss of arable land, drives many Bangladeshis to choose exile.

Another wall inextricably connected to the climate crisis is the barrier separating the USA from Mexico. The development of Mexico's coastal regions – as part of a perspective of industrialization and building the tourism sector – also means massive volumes of pollutants being poured into the oceans. These pollutants drive the proliferation of toxic algae, which in turn endanger fish stocks.[102] Fishermen and peasants have the choice of either indebting themselves in order to survive, or else migrating north, to the USA. Pollution, migration and debt in this sense mutually reinforce one another.

Nuclear deterrence and ecological crisis

Militaries are interested in what form the logic of climate change will take, just as they were concerned with the logic of nuclear deterrence in the Cold War period. We cannot understand anything about how game theory developed in the postwar period if we do not see how this discipline contributed to feeding Pentagon strategists' thinking.

The logic of climate change is different in nature to the logic of nuclear deterrence. During the Cold War, the US armed forces were wholly focused on the objective of avoiding a nuclear war with the Soviets and, if such conflict did nonetheless occur, having the capability to react in an appropriate manner.

Such a confrontation was unlikely, considering that the two superpowers both owned powerful nuclear arsenals and, indeed, no such conflict ever did take place. US military figures were conscious of the weak likelihood of a nuclear war with the USSR. If, despite everything, this possibility did structure the organization of the US armed forces across half a century, that was because the consequences if it had happened would have been devastating.[103] A nuclear conflict would have affected all aspects of social life and in lasting fashion. The logic of nuclear deterrence was underpinned by the weak probability of war breaking out, but major consequences if it did.

The logic of climate change is a wholly different one. The probability of this change occurring is very high indeed and, even today, we can see its first consequences. Even supposing that the industrialized countries did decide to act, the effects of their actions would not make themselves felt for several years or decades. Unlike in the case of a nuclear attack, the consequences of the ecological crisis are difficult to evaluate. Certainly these effects will not be distributed in a homogeneous manner – they will not affect all continents in the same fashion. Even if a nuclear attack can wreak destruction across an entire region, it occurs in a given space-time. Conversely, climate change proceeds gradually. Or more precisely, some of its aspects, like ice melting or temperatures rising, are gradual. Others, however, like hurricanes and droughts, are circumscribed in space and time. Climate change very probably will happen, but its consequences are very hard to evaluate; in some places it will have an immense impact, whereas it will leave others almost unperturbed.

Moreover, a nuclear attack is underpinned by the logic of the enemy's intentionality. This implies that the theory of rationality applies here, in the sense that it is – at least in theory – possible to understand and anticipate the enemy's intentionality and to negotiate with him. Indeed, the specific focus of one of Thomas Schelling's major works, *The Strategy of Conflict*, is the possible variety of such interactions among belligerents.[104] Even if it is more difficult to grasp the intentions of a terrorist network like Al-Qaeda, on account of its nebulous character – in the sense that its command structure is not very centralized – it, too, has a certain rationality. Conversely, nature in general and environmental change in particular are not underpinned by any kind of intentionality. Nature is not a conventional enemy that has a plan, identifiable interests and chosen spokespersons. Besides, it is not in fact an enemy at all. This means that the element of foresight or anticipation is difficult to apply, or in any case, not of the same order.

Climate change is the fruit of human activities. That is what gives meaning to the expression 'Anthropocene'; a term that Nobel chemistry laureate Paul Crutzen coined in the 2000s and which has been a resounding success since then.[105] This expression refers to a geological period following on from the Holocene at the end of the eighteenth century. The Anthropocene is the period in which humanity becomes a decisive geophysical power, bearing effects on the biosphere itself. The histories of humanity and nature become more and more interlinked, to the point that they can no longer be considered in separation from one another. However, this does not make them any easier to understand. The logic of 'unintended consequences' classically described by Raymond Boudon fully applies here: the macroscopic consequences of human actions are by definition hard to predict, since the aggregation of numerous actions 'deviates' the various actors' initial intentions.[106] When this aggregation includes not only social processes but also natural ones, the 'deviation' brings consequences that are even more unexpected. From this derives the difficulty in anticipating climate change and the possibilities of 'non-linear' phenomena occurring, as causes of (seemingly) limited importance lead to the most extraordinary consequences.

War and biofuels

Militaries' preoccupation with climate change comes in a context in which fossil fuels have become far more expensive. A series of articles appearing in *Armed Forces Journal*, the US officers' monthly, have expressed concerns in this regard. The armed forces account for 80 per cent of the oil consumed by the US state,[107] requiring 130 million barrels a year in order to function. Oil today represents 77 per cent of the fuel that the armed forces use and it makes up 70 per cent of the overall tonnage delivered to their battlefields.[108] Fuel and water together make up 90 per cent of overall tonnage; by comparison munitions constitute a relatively modest percentage. More generally, 10 per cent of carbon emissions worldwide come from military activity (adding together all the world's armed forces).[109] The US armed forces' oil consumption is self-reinforcing in character. Large numbers of personnel have to be mobilized in order to secure the routes for delivering oil to theatres of operations like Iraq, where one of the main tactics used by the insurgents is to try to prevent its smooth passage. These personnel themselves need oil, which further adds to overall consumption. Each day 2.5 million gallons of oil are transported to Iraq, in highly dangerous conditions.[110]

As militaries see things, this situation is an untenable one – and for several reasons. Western armies' dependence on oil places them at the mercy of producer countries with whom they have bad relations, first among them Iran and Venezuela. Another supplier to the USA, Mexico, is in a situation of quasi-civil war on account of narcotrafficking.

Indeed, narcotraffickers frequently attack oil pipelines.[111] At the beginning of the 1980s, President Carter formulated a doctrine that still today takes his name, the 'Carter Doctrine', stipulating that the United States would intervene militarily wherever its energy supply channels are threatened. This particularly applied to the Middle East, where two-thirds of known oil reserves are located. However, the doctrine is becoming more and more difficult to put into effect. The 'imperial overstretch' that blights the US armed forces weakens its capacity to react to newly arising geopolitical crises. That is why calls for a diversification of fuels and energy sources are being made within the armed forces themselves.

This is not the first time that the US armed forces have mounted far-reaching transitions in their technological and energy policies. From the mid nineteenth century up till the interwar period, coal was the dominant energy source used by the military. Oil gradually came to replace coal, as its civilian use became generalized. Then came nuclear energy, used in the production of bombs and in marine and submarine propulsion. Neither of these transitions was carried out because the previous energy source was exhausted, but rather on account of economic and political choices.[112] In parallel to this, since the 1940s armed forces have ever more relied on electronics and IT in both their logistics and their weaponry.

Weapons that are being conceived today will only become available for use in forty or fifty years' time. As such, it is crucial that armed forces begin – even now – to prepare for that future.[113] One objective advanced by the *Armed Forces Journal* holds that the Pentagon should be able to make all its systems work with non-oil-based fuels – and in particular, with biofuels – by 2040. The first 'hybrid' warship – the *USS Makin Islands*, which is propelled by gas and electricity – deployed in 2009. Military bases will also have to invest in solar, geothermal and wind energy.

An economic argument is often used to prove the necessity of this energy transition. The US armed forces' use of biofuels will create massive demand, which will lighten producers' uncertainties over the viability of this sector and encourage them to increase production. The armed forces' conversion will give a green light to the market, encouraging society as a whole to carry out this transition. American military figures tend to consider themselves 'pathfinders' guiding the way to energy transition. And they would be wrong to pass up such a role. Year after year, when the US population is surveyed on what institution it has most confidence in, it places the military first on the list (except for a brief period during the war in Iraq). Next come small businesses, the police and organized religion.[114] The militarization of ecology could thus convince hitherto reticent sections of US society to accept certain energy transition measures.

Militaries' conversion to biofuels will create major problems. In recent years, the increasing tendency to devote arable land to producing biofuels has led to a rise in the cost of agricultural products, since this land is no longer available for growing food. To fill a large car's fueltank with ethanol is equivalent to using up the same volume of corn it would take to feed a person for a year. [115] Sating the military's thirst for biofuels will unavoidably aggravate this tendency. It is also possible that the increasing scarcity of fossil fuels will drive an increased recourse to nuclear energy and that further proliferation will follow. Moreover, the oil industry – which has congenital ties to the military-industrial complex – is far from having admitted defeat. Some people think that we are seeing the emergence of a 'new age of hydrocarbons', rather than an era based on alternative energy sources.[116] US domestic fossil fuel production has also recently increased. Deepwater drilling (for example in Brazil), shale gas (of which the US has large reserves) and oil sands (especially in Canada) all mean an unexpected abundance of fossil fuels, pushing down prices and increasing consumption. Different factions of the ruling classes in the West are clashing over these alternative plans for energy use. These contradictions also run through militaries themselves.

The oceans destabilized

Navies are particularly concerned by the ecological crisis. The oceans have always been dangerous environments. As we saw in Chapter 2, modern insurance is in part the child of seventeenth-century seafaring, when insurance was provided for the assets that would be lost in case of shipwreck. Advances in cartography and transport technology helped to stabilize this environment in the following centuries, to the point that it soon became the main vector of globalization. Today, 90 per cent of global trade is fulfilled by sea.

However, climate change risks destabilizing the oceans anew. The oceans are not a homogeneous mass, but moving organisms composed of water columns of variable density, salinity, temperature and acidity. Climate change is already upsetting thermohaline circulation, namely the ocean currents that move across the world, the best known of which is the Gulf Stream. The existing currents, which are a vital factor in submarine navigation, may therefore be weakened, or even change direction.[117] This will demand more frequent charting and sampling of the oceans. As one military report has it, until now the oceans had been 'stationary' in character – that is, they changed but within fixed parameters.[118] Today, climate change is putting these parameters themselves in question.

Melting ice changes the water's density and this risks compromising submarines' stability. In 1999, the US nuclear sub *USS Hawkbill* reported that changes in the salinity of the water and corresponding variations in the density of the currents made it more difficult for it to maintain a steady buoyancy.[119] The increase in the sea's acidity on account of rising carbon dioxide levels will also have effects on submarines' sonar systems. Sea currents have certain acoustic properties that make it possible to predict how sound waves spread out. Since the Second World War, submarines have been equipped with sensor systems, whose operation is based on this predictability. These systems played a particularly crucial role in submarine conflict during the Cold War.[120] Changes in water density may complicate the future functioning of these sonars. Ice melting in the Arctic, as well as humanity's own presence making itself felt, will increase ambient underwater noise in certain regions, making sonar detection more difficult.

Problems of this kind will also be posed at surface level. During the second Gulf War, extreme heat prevented the personnel working on the US aircraft carriers' bridges from remaining exposed to the sun for too long.[121] This meant slowing the rhythm of fighter planes taking off. Environmental change aggravates extreme climates and this makes soldiers' tasks both physically and psychologically more difficult. It will also have an impact on military materiel and infrastructure, subject to high temperatures and very strong winds. During each of the Iraq wars, the cost of maintaining military equipment increased, on account of desert sandstorms. If the ice melting in the Arctic will make it possible to cross this region by sea at certain times of year, the problem is that electronics systems are not necessarily adapted to the extreme cold; and making them so is very expensive. As the French parliamentary report mentioned above summarizes, 'Changes in the climate have repercussions for equipment and weapons systems. These latter may deterioriate due to raised temperatures and high humidity. Radar performance may be affected. There may be anomalies in how sound waves spread out. When new weapons are built, this will have to take into account climatic developments. Combatants' clothing will also have to be adapted to the new and specific circumstances of different kinds of battlefield.'[122]

The scramble for the Arctic

Any document devoted to the military consequences of climate change will doubtless include a section on the Arctic. The military mind's fascination for the North Pole knows no equivalent, save for the uncertainties surrounding the political and economic consequences of global warming for this region. The Antarctic does not exert the same seductive power, because it is at some distance from the main sea routes and the conflicts that structured the twentieth century (and promise to define the twenty-first). It is not only military figures who are fascinated by the Arctic. James Lovelock, father of 'Gaia theory', hypothesized in a 2006 *Independent* column that when global warming reaches unsustainable levels the last surviving humans will move to take refuge in the Arctic.[123]

One thing is certain: the Arctic is melting and increasingly quickly. A NASA-financed study published in early 2011 tells us that in 2006 alone the two poles decreased by 475 billion tonnes of ice.[124] Since 1992, the rate at which the poles are melting has increased by 36 billion tonnes each year. Among other disastrous consequences, this will contribute to sea levels rising 15 cm by 2050, to which we must add other glaciers melting, as well as the oceans expanding as their temperatures rise. Since records began in the 1950s, temperatures have increased in the Arctic twice as quickly as the global average (mean) rate. Almost all the glaciers there are shrinking. The speed at which it is getting warmer is particularly explained by the 'albedo effect'. Ice melting into water makes the Earth's surface darker; where ice and snow had once reflected the sun's rays, the ocean absorbs more heat, which causes more warming at a local level, which melts more ice . . . and so on. This melting is particularly notable in permafrost – the Arctic soils that do not thaw even in summer – and this could release massive quantities of the greenhouse gas methane into the atmosphere.

This military fascination for the Arctic is not a new phenomenon. During the Cold War, the North Pole was the obsession of the world's major armed forces and in particular the US and Soviet militaries.[125] A significant part of the scientific knowledge concerning this region first originated from research programmes financed by the US armed forces.[126] Launching a guided missile or navigating a deep-sea submarine requires mastering the environmental conditions in which they are operated. That is particularly true in a hostile environment like the Arctic. As a 1950 US military study devoted to the Arctic explains, 'emphasis must be accorded those unique environmental features that presently impose the chief obstacles to the conduct of military operations'.[127]

The attention that the Americans devoted to the Arctic during the Cold War is not hard to explain. Alaska and Siberia are border regions, separated by the Bering Straits. The shortest route for Soviet bombers or missiles to reach American metropoles passed via the North Pole. American strategists also contemplated the possibility of the Arctic becoming the theatre of a 'hot' war between the superpowers. This implied the need to prepare equipment and tactics appropriate to this environment. At the time it was accepted that the Soviets were more advanced than the Americans, in this regard.

As such, in the late 1940s, meetings dedicated to the Arctic were held at the Pentagon. In the late 1950s, shortly after the Russians launched Sputnik (in 1957), the *USS Nautilus* – so named in homage to Jules Verne – became the first submarine to voyage under the Arctic ice cap. The first hypotheses that scientists provided to explain of Arctic ice melting date back to the 1930s. From the 1940s onward, military figures became conscious of the climate change involved and the fact that this would make military manoeuvres all the more difficult.[128] This moment also saw the launch of research programmes regarding melting ice, sea currents, the chemical composition of the water, salinity, mountains and valleys under the water and so on.

The North Pole and globalization

The Cold War is over, but militaries are still interested in the Arctic. The fact that the ice is melting at an accelerated rate, combined with the geopolitical and economic upheavals of recent decades, has changed the situation in the region. Since 2007, the Northwest Passage linking the Atlantic and the Pacific has been wholly open for two weeks a year, and some predict that in coming years it may be open for the whole summer. In August 2009 two German commercial ships, which were not accompanied by icebreakers, took the Northeast Passage (or the 'Northern Sea Route') along the northern coast of Siberia, reaching the Netherlands having started out from Vladivostok.[129] This passage is now open for four or five months a year. In 2010 only four vessels took this route, but thirty-four did so in 2012, including a cruise ship.[130] In 2009, six thousand vessels navigated the Arctic (in a broad sense), most of them fishing trawlers and mining barges.

The fact that the Arctic is becoming negotiable does not mean that it will be *easily* negotiable in the near future. This remains an inhospitable region and icebergs and other moving ice can potentially inflict major damage on seaborn vessels. Given that it is difficult to predict how the ice moves, journey times promise to vary wildly. Moreover, the cartography of the Arctic is still imprecise, compared to other regions. These various factors will translate into higher insurance premiums, which is itself a symptom of the risks involved. This will also mean that vessels will often have to be escorted by ice-breakers. All the same, the increasing negotiability of the Arctic will have a considerable economic and geopolitical impact. As testament to this, the liberal weekly *The Economist* – the world's most influential newspaper, never late in responding to a new discovery – recently devoted one of its 'special reports' to the Arctic.[131]

Within fifteen to twenty years the navigability of Arctic sea routes will have become an enduring reality and journey times from continent to continent will be sharply reduced. This will reduce the quantities of fuel used and the price of the commodities transported and – all other things being equal – accelerate globalization. Ships that today travel from Rotterdam to Yokohama – both of them cargo ports of global importance – via the Suez Canal will have 40 per cent shorter journeys when they instead take the Northeast Passage. Navigating from Seattle to Rotterdam through the Northwest Passage, rather than via the Panama Canal, will mean a 25 per cent faster journey.[132] The expressions 'new Baltic Sea', 'new Mediterranean' and 'new Gulf of Mexico' often recur in the literature devoted to the Arctic. This change in sea trade routes is not good news for everyone. Today Egypt takes in five billion dollars in transit tolls a year thanks to the Suez Canal – a figure that will inevitably decline as shorter and cheaper alternatives emerge.

Five countries have sovereignty claims in the Arctic: the USA, Russia, Denmark (via Greenland), Norway and Canada. These countries, together with Finland, Sweden and Iceland, make up the Arctic Council, an intergovernmental forum founded in 1996, which is responsible for handling conflicts in the region. The Council also has NGOs as members, notably including the WWF, but not Greenpeace, whose involvement was barred. Some of these NGOs represent the rights of indigenous populations living in the Arctic, including the Inuits.

These countries have conflicts over territory in the Arctic. In July 2007 a Russian submarine expedition planted a titanium flag on the Lomonosov ridge, 4,000 m beneath the North Pole, amid great publicity. Russia considers this ridge an underwater extension of its territory. The UN Convention on the Law of the Sea (UNCLOS), agreed in the 1970s, stipulates that any country that can demonstrate that its continental shelf extends more than 200 nautical miles beyond its shoreline has rights over exploiting the resources found there.[133] The Lomonosov ridge is probably rich in minerals and oil, hence Russia's eagerness to establish its control. The attractiveness of this region is also explained by the fact that with global warming certain species (notably fish) are migrating further north.

Denmark and Canada each contest Russia's claims to this territory. While the Danes maintain that the ridge is an extension of Greenland, the Canadians insist that it is Canada's. The fact that the Arctic is a circle makes such a disagreement difficult to resolve from a geographical point of view. The most pessimistic commentators fear that this kind of territorial conflict may in future lead to warfare.[134] Their perspective sees the division of the Arctic through the prism of the nineteenth-century scramble for Africa – that is to say, it is likely to give rise to new forms of inter-imperialist conflict.

At this stage, the fear of major conflicts emerging in the Arctic seems unfounded. Ninety per cent of the metal ores found in the Arctic are situated within uncontested borders.[135] Moreover, in such a hostile environment, inter-state cooperation is more rational than conflict. That is not to say that we can rule out such a risk for the decades to come. In 2011 the Canadian army carried out the largest military exercise in its history in this region.[136] The Russians militarily dominate the North Pole, also because they have over twenty ice-breakers, some of which are nuclear-propelled (the first nuclear-propelled ice-breaker was built in the late 1950s and was called the *Lenin*). By comparison, the USA only has three vessels of this kind.[137] Building a latest-generation ice-breaker takes between eight and ten years and costs a billion dollars. One of the US military's insistent demands is to overcome this gap in military capacity in coming years; but the fiscal crisis hitting the United States hardly seems conducive to the kind of investment that achieving such an objective would require.

Arctic geopolitics are a matter of interest for countries far beyond those who have territorial claims in the region. The great Asian exporters – China, Japan, South Korea, Singapore

– have asked to join the Arctic Council and there is a good chance that they will be accepted into it in the next few years. Given that these countries count among the main beneficiaries of the shortening of trade routes, it is hardly surprising that they take a close interest in the Arctic. South Korea is one of the world's main ice-breaker producers. For their part, India, China and Japan regularly finance scientific missions to the North Pole.

The melting of the Arctic ice will also have indirect geopolitical consequences, since it promises to alter the importance of certain strategic hubs. For instance, a large proportion of the commodities heading to – and coming from – Asia, a third of total world trade, pass through the Strait of Malacca, situated between Malaysia and the Indonesian island of Sumatra. Guaranteeing the security of this strait has for centuries proven rather a conundrum. Since the origins of international trade, the strait has been infested with pirates. Moreover, China's emergence as a world power and its mounting rivalry with the United States risk fuelling the struggle for military supremacy in the area, as well as in the China Sea, to which it offers access.

The Strait of Hormuz, running between Iran and the Sultanate of Oman, is another point of geostrategic and commercial fixations of this same kind. Allowing trade and military vessels to avoid taking this route would considerably reduce Iran's influence over any Middle-East crisis. As such, opening the Arctic sea routes will ultimately shuffle the cards of world geopolitics. It will reduce the pressure exerted in certain other locations, increase it in others and, in so doing, it will change power relations and the configuration of alliances.

Commodifying the thaw

The Arctic is home to abundant natural resources and the economic benefits of the ice melting do not only flow out of the shortening of trade routes. Wood, minerals, zinc, gold and nickel in particular; but also oil, gas, fish, plants . . . It is believed that the region contains the world's last hydrocarbon reserves. According to a 2008 study, the Arctic is home to 90 billion barrels of oil and 75 trillion m³ of natural gas, potentially amounting to 13 and 30 per cent of still-unexplored resources, respectively.[138] The likes of Shell, ExxonMobil, Gazprom and Total are already spending billions on such exploration (in Total's case, just for gas). Shell alone has spent $4bn in the Arctic. In September 2015, the company announced that it was abandoning drilling operations in the Arctic for the 'forseeable future'. How long this decision will last will in good part be determined by the trajectory of the oil market. The exploitation of resources in the Arctic demands setting up large-scale, sophisticated infrastructure, as well as securing their transportation. This securitization is one of the reasons that will drive military involvement in the region. Oil companies' own involvement is very much dependent on the price of a barrel of oil. In the 1980s, when the price fluctuated around $15 a barrel, it was unprofitable to take the risk of exploiting Arctic wells, but with a price of $100 and more, as it is today, it does become worthwhile. Moreover, oil is not the only natural resource whose price has increased in recent years. This is also true of numerous metal ores and rare-earth minerals and this rise promises to encourage mining activity in the region.

Oil exploitation in the region entails numerous risks. Cleaning up oil spills is always a difficult task. The explosion of BP's (British Petroleum) 'Deepwater Horizon' oil rig in the Gulf of Mexico in April 2010 – the greatest catastrophe in the industry's history – proved disastrous from every point of view. Over three months more than 800 million litres of oil were discharged into the Gulf. Given the inhospitable character of the Arctic environment, it seems difficult to imagine rig repair operations or trying to save affected wildlife in such a context.

The Arctic thaw raises unprecedented problems of sovereignty. Conflicts relating to the delimitation of national borders, as mentioned above, are one such problem. There is also a risk of a rise of econationalism, as is often the case when new natural resources are discovered. The Inuits of the countries surrounding the North Pole have since 1977 organized the 'Inuit Circumpolar Council' in order to assert their rights to the Arctic's natural resources.[139] This council brings together the Inuits of Denmark, Canada, the United States and Russia. In a 2009 statement, it proclaimed 'It is our right to freely determine our political status, freely pursue our economic, social, cultural and linguistic development and freely dispose of our natural wealth and resource.' As we have seen, modern nationalism is always linked to a certain representation of nature; of natural/national heritage. Greenland is itself considering demanding independence from Denmark. With global warming, this region could see a considerable development of agriculture in coming decades. The years to come could also see large quantities of hydroelectric energy being harvested there.[140]

The speed of the circulation of capital

Capitalism must constantly seek 'the annihilation of space by time'; that is, create transport and communications technologies allowing it to realize more surplus-value in ever-new regions of the world. As Karl Marx said, 'while capital must on one side strive to tear down every spatial barrier to intercourse, to exchange and conquer the whole earth for its market, it strives on the other side to annihilate this space with time, that is, to reduce to a minimum the time spent in motion from one place to another. The more developed the capital, therefore, the more extensive the market over which it circulates, which forms the spatial orbit of its circulation, the more does it strive simultaneously for an even greater extension of the market and for greater annihilation of space by time.'[141]

Capital has an inherent tendency to conquer the world as a whole and turn it into a market. Marx writes in a passage in *Capital* that 'the world market is contained in the very notion of capital'. But capitalism's global expansion comes at a price. The greater the distance between the commodity's site of production and the site of its sale (of its 'realization' as a commodity), the more its cost increases – after all, transport isn't free. This implies that capitalism must constantly accelerate commodities' 'speed of circulation', in order to minimize their transport costs and maximize the profits that capitalists draw from them. The profits that they pocket depend on this speed increasing. That is what Marx means by the 'annihilation of space by time'. Since the nineteenth century, it has been possible to accelerate the speed of capital circulation by using fossil fuels – coal and then oil – which have served to propel ever-faster means of transport: trains, cars, boats, planes . . .[142]

Following in the wake of Marx, David Harvey has drawn attention to one of capitalism's modes of crisis resolution, which he refers to using the concept of the 'spatial fix'. This has two meanings, one of them literal, the other metaphorical. The literal one refers to the idea that capitalism is a spatial entity, which takes over – fixes itself in – its environment and transforms it. It materializes in machines, means of transport and modes of communication. The metaphorical meaning of the concept instead refers to the idea of 'solving' the problem of the crisis; but this is a solution that, like taking drugs (a 'fix' in the sense of a 'dose'), is only a temporary and illusory one. One of the ways in which capital resolves crises is spatial in character – more precisely, it moves capitals to what were previously 'virgin lands' lacking capitalist relations. This concept of the 'spatial fix' allows Harvey to argue that what Marx called 'primitive accumulation' is not only 'primitive', in the sense of characterizing the early days of capitalism. It is repeated in cycles across the course of history, each time that a crisis of capital over-accumulation has to be resolved.

With the climate crisis, the 'annihilation of space by time' reaches a new stage of its history, such as not even Marx could have predicted.[143] Capitalism is still capitalism and, as such, it is irremediably subject to crises, which it can temporarily overcome through spatial fixes. But this process is now caught up with environmental phenomena, which it will seek to profit from by taking up the opportunities that are thus provided. What we are today seeing in the Arctic thus owes to both very old and very new tendencies. Old ones, in that the scramble for the Arctic is underpinned by the centuries-old logic of capitalist profit. New ones, in that this logic is now mixed with another one – the logic of climate change. Future crises of capitalism will be inextricably both economic and ecological. They will only more clearly show the need to establish a link between ecology and critique of the capitalist system.

Conclusion

The classical Marxists – Engels, Lenin, Trotsky, Gramsci, Mao . . . – took military strategists very seriously. Clausewitz's *oeuvre* bore particularly considerable impact on the strategies deployed by the workers' movement from the last quarter of the nineteenth century onward and numerous Marxists produced interpretations of his work.[144] As Carl Schmitt explains in his *Theory of the Partisan*, Lenin's reading of Clausewitz was one of the most important political events of the modern era.

Since the 1920s, the attention that critical theorists have devoted to military strategy has been rather less pronounced. One of the characteristics of 'Western' Marxism – in the period between 1924 and 1968[145] – was its lack of interest in strategic questions and weak acquaintance with military doctrine. None of the main leading lights of critical thinking today – Badiou, Žižek, Jameson, Butler, Fraser . . . – are reading military strategists, either past or present. Michael Hardt's and Toni Negri's work is a relatively exceptional case, in that they briefly refer to the 'Revolution in military affairs' (RMA) in their book *Multitude*. This consideration ought to be set in relation to the general poverty of strategic reflection in current-day critical theories. However interesting they are, they often settle for abstractions of very little political substance.

What lessons can critical theories draw from today's military strategists and, in particular, what analyses that concern the military implications of ecological crisis? Without doubt, it is too early to say. However, if, as Clausewitz thought, every society has its own way of making war, studying military strategy is a necessary path to go down in order to understand and transform the society that we are living in.

Conclusion: Game Over?

'The experience of our generation: that capitalism will not die a natural death.'[1] With these words from his *Arcades Project* – providing the epigraph to our book – Walter Benjamin targeted the 'historicism' so dominant in the Marxism of his time. Whatever their differences, the Marxisms of the Second and Third Internationals each considered themselves to be on the 'right' side of history, swimming with the current of history. The socialization of the productive forces and technical development would inevitably lead humanity towards socialism, whatever the peripeties encountered along the way. In this sense, they considered capitalism doomed to die 'a natural death' under the weight of its own contradictions. Paradoxically, the tone-deafness of the revolutionary Left faced with fascism originated in this 'optimism'. As they saw it, fascism was a barbarism from the past that would rapidly disappear; one that would not, in any case, be able to change the strategic situation in any deep sense. Walter Benjamin counterposed to this historicism the 'experience' of his generation, the generation that fell victim to fascism. Capitalism would not die of its own accord; it would have to be put to death through revolutionaries' activity. If this system has proven to have one characteristic, it is its stunning resilience – its capacity constantly to reinvent itself in order to surmount its crises.

The Arcades Project was written between 1927 and 1940. Three-quarters of a century later, Benjamin's comment takes on another meaning. Firstly, it does so because contemporary critical thought has renounced any sense of optimism. After the tragedies of the twentieth century, it is instead pessimism that rules. Currently the question is rather more that of whether revolutionary forces are capable of carrying forth a project of radical social change, or if such a project instead now belongs to the past.

Moreover, the 'natural death' to which Benjamin refers takes on fresh meaning in these times of environmental crisis. The capitalist exploitation of nature has reached such a degree, after two centuries, that we could imagine this system leading to its own self-destruction. The exhaustion of resources and the growing costs associated with managing the negative consequences that this has for development are bearing increasing pressure on capitalist value formation. And they endanger the very conditions of life on Earth.

In recent decades, recognition of these facts has given rise to a new 'historicism'. This is a historicism that places its confidence not in the direction of history, as the Second and Third Internationals once did, but in the environmental crisis getting its own back on the modern world (be it called 'capitalism' or otherwise), once and for all. This 'catastrophist' belief has numerous expressions in today's ecologist movements and ecologist thinking.[2] For example, certain 'degrowth' currents more or less explicitly subscribe to this argument, as does Jared Diamond – in a different form – in his neo-Malthusian best-sellers.[3] Its connotation has changed but the idea remains the same: something in the very logic of the system will lead to its disappearance. In this case, we are not talking about the socialization of the productive forces or about technical development, but the over-exploitation of nature, which dooms capitalism to certain death.

The book that you have just read shows the degree to which this catastrophism is mistaken. Capitalism will not die a natural death, for one simple reason: it has the means to adapt to the environmental crisis. It is about to show its stunning resilience once again. In the last instance, the financialization and militarization of this crisis are nothing but illustrations of such a conclusion. In truth, capitalism is not only capable of adapting to the environmental crisis, but – on top of that – of profiting from it. Indeed, there is no prior guarantee that the ecological crisis will aggravate the economic crisis. On the contrary, it will perhaps allow capitalism to find lasting solutions to the falling rate of profit, commodifying sectors of social and natural life that have up till now been protected from the logic of capital. One crisis thus serves to resolve another.

In his *Prison Notebooks*, Antonio Gramsci, another victim of the tragic 'experience' of which Walter Benjamin spoke, asked why all the revolutionary processes arising in Western Europe in the 1920s in the wake of the Russian Revolution ended in failure. In Germany, Hungary and Italy, powerful movements emerged in response to the hope born in the East, but all of them were rapidly defeated. In Gramsci's eyes, the answer lay in the different structure of 'Western' societies and 'Oriental' societies such as Tsarist Russia: in the East, he said,

> the State was everything, civil society was primordial and gelatinous; in the West, there was a proper relationship between State and civil society and when the State trembled, a sturdy structure of civil society was at once revealed. The State was only an outer ditch, behind which there was a powerful system of fortresses and earthworks . . .[4]

What Gramsci said with regard to the link between civil society and the state in the West can also be said with regard to the relation between capitalism and nature: they are separated by 'earthworks' and 'fortresses'. In the modern era, the relationship between capitalism and nature is never an immediate one. The state exercises an intermediary or interface role in between the two. Under the capitalist system, the relation between capital accumulation and nature is always mortgaged or articulated by the state. Why so? Because the logic of capital is blind and without limit. Left to its own devices, it draws profit from the resources available to it – natural resources, as well as other kinds – to the point of their exhaustion. It is, moreover, incapable of handling the harmful effects of the production process: pollutions, stocks being used up, damage to human health, economic crises, conflicts . . . The state instead has to deal with all this. Regulating access to resources and taking responsibility for the negative consequences of development, it works in the ruling classes' long-term interests and allows the sustained exploitation of nature.

The capitalist state nonetheless also has the function of constructing nature, as we saw in Chapter 2. If it is to be exploited in lasting fashion, this requires that it first be organized or 'configured'. For example, at the legal level, the state issues property rights over natural species or CO_2 particles and thus authorizes private operators to profit from marketing them. Or at the statistical level; accounting for and administering natural resources has been an obsession of the state's at least since the physiocrats of the eighteenth century (and physiocrat means 'government by nature'). As such, the state organizes nature and places it at capital's disposal. The generation of capitalist value demands a ceaseless production and destruction of nature. Capital does not achieve this alone, however; it needs the help of a body upon which it can confer tasks that it is not itself able to accomplish – the state. In the modern era, capitalism, nature and the state thus constitute an indissociable triptych.

So what alternative is there to 'catastrophism'? The answer is the same one today as it was in Walter Benjamin's time: to politicize the crisis. To put that another way: to pull apart the triptych of capitalism, nature and the state and to prevent this latter working in the interests of capital. That is exactly what the environmental justice movement managed to do when it coined the concept of 'environmental racism', recognizing that the state's toxic-waste management policies systematically favour White and well-off populations. In so doing, it unleashed a powerful social movement.

Notes

Introduction

1 See Eileen Maura McGurty, 'From NIMBY to civil rights. The origins of the environmental justice movement', *Environmental History*, 2 (3), 1997.

2 Marianne Chaumel and Stéphane La Branche, 'Inégalités écologiques: vers quelle définition?', *Espace, populations, sociétés*, 1, 2008, p. 107.

3 Nicolas Hulot, *Pour un pacte écologique*, Calmann-Lévy, Paris, 2006.

4 Dipesh Chakrabarty, *Provincializing Europe: Postcolonial Thought and Historical Difference*, Princeton University Press, Princeton, NJ, 2000.

5 Dipesh Chakrabarty, 'The Climate of History. Four Theses', *Critical Inquiry*, 35, Winter 2009.

6 Ibid., p. 221. See also 'Penser et agir en tant qu'espèce. Entretien avec Dipesh Chakrabarty', interview by Razmig Keucheyan, Charlotte Nordmann and Julien Vincent, *Revue des livres*, 8, November–December 2012.

7 Ibid., p. 217.

8 Chakrabarty has explained himself on this point: see Dipesh Chakrabarty, 'Postcolonial studies and the challenge of climate change', *New Literary History*, 41 (1), Winter 2012.

9 Alexandre Jaunait and Sébastien Chauvin, 'Représenter l'intersection. Les théories de l'intersectionnalité à l'épreuve des sciences sociales', *Revue française de science politique*, 62 (1), 2012.

10 The interlacing of financialization and war is at the heart of the *longue-durée* periodization of capitalism that Giovanni Arrighi proposes in his *The Long Twentieth Century. Money, Power, and the Origins of our Time*, Verso, London, 2009.

11 Karl Marx and Friedrich Engels, *The Manifesto of the Communist Party*, in *Marx-Engels Collected Works*, Vol. 6, Lawrence and Wishart, London, 1976 [1848], p. 487.

12 Before we begin we shall make a terminological clarification. The notion of 'ecological crisis' or 'environmental crisis' frequently used in this work designates a complex tangle of natural and social processes that are currently at work. We will leave to one side the many epistemological questions that this definition raises.

1 Environmental Racism

1 For an overview of these movements, see ch. 17 of Kenneth A. Gould and Tammy L. Lewis (eds.), *Twenty Lessons in Environmental Sociology*, Oxford University Press, Oxford, 2008.

2 See Joan Martinez Alier, *The Environmentalism of the Poor. A Study of Ecological Conflicts and Valuation*, Edward Elgar, Northampton, 2003. For a recent perspective on environmental conflicts in Latin America see Maristella Svampa, 'Néo-"développementalisme" extractiviste, gouvernements et mouvements sociaux en Amérique latine', *Problèmes d'Amérique latine*, 81, Summer 2011.

3 'For a mass of people to be led to think coherently and in the same coherent fashion about the real present world, is a "philosophical" event far more important and "original" than the discovery by some philosophical "genius" of a truth which remains the property of small groups of intellectuals': Antonio Gramsci, *Selections From the Prison Notebooks*, Lawrence and Wishart, London, 1971, p. 325.

4 See Anthony Oberschall, *Social Conflicts and Social Movements*, Prentice Hall, Englewood Cliffs, 1973.

5 See Éloi Laurent, 'Écologie et inégalités', *Revue de l'OFCE*, 109/2, 2009.

6 Peter Newell provides a discussion of multinational companies' strategies for locating polluting industries: see his 'Race, class and the global politics of environmental inequality', *Global Environmental Politics*, 5 (3), August 2005. On the history of waste incinerators in France, see Stéphane Frioux and Isabelle Roussel, 'L'incinération des déchets, bienfait sanitaire? De l'ère hygiéniste à

la crise de la dioxine (1890–1990)', *Environnement, Risques et Santé*, 11 (5), September–October 2012.

7 See its website: www.sierraclub.org. On the history of nature protection societies in France from the nineteenth century onward, see for instance Stephanie Pinceti, 'Some origins of French environmentalism. An explortion', *Forest and Conservation History*, 37, April 1993.

8 See Giovanna di Chiro, 'Nature as community. The convergence of environment and social justice', in William Cronon (ed.), *Uncommon Ground. Rethinking the Human Place in Nature*, WW Norton, New York, 1996, p. 299.

9 See Eileen Maura McGurty, 'From NIMBY to civil rights. The origins of the environmental justice movement', loc. cit., p. 304.

10 Robert D. Bullard, *Dumping in Dixie. Race, Class and Environmental Quality*, Westview Press, Boulder, 2000.

11 For example, on the French case see Florian Charvolin, *L'Invention de l'environnement en France. Chronique anthropologique d'une institutionnalisation*, La Découverte, Paris, 2009.

12 See Andrew Szasz, *Ecopopulism. Toxic Waste and the Movement for Environmental Justice*, University of Minnesota Press, Minneapolis, 1994.

13 François Gemenne, *Géopolitique du changement climatique*, Armand Colin, Paris, 2009, pp. 73–74. See also Romain Huret, *Katrina 2005, L'ouragan, l'État et les pauvres aux États-Unis*, Éditions de l'EHESS, Paris, 2010.

14 Harald Welzer, *Climate Wars. Why People will be Killed in the Twenty-First Century*, Polity, Cambridge, 2012, p. 25.

15 Naomi Klein, *The Shock Doctrine: The Rise of Disaster Capitalism*, Metropolitan Books/Henry Holt, New York, 2007.

16 Patrick Sharkey, 'Survival and death in New Orleans. An empirical look at the human impact of Katrina', *Journal of Black Studies*, 37 (4), 2007.

17 Ibid., p. 490.

18 See Robert D. Bullard et al., *Toxic Waste and Race at Twenty, 1987–2007*, United Church of Christ, Cleveland, March 2007.

19 Ibid., p. 131.

20 Laura Pulido, 'Rethinking environmental racism. White privilege and urban development in Southern California', *Annals of the Association of American Geographers*, 90 (1), 2000, p. 16.

21 In the sense of a Marxist 'real abstraction', a theme we will introduce in Chapter 2 (see pp. 81–5).

22 Pulido, 'Rethinking environmental racism …' p. 31.

23 For one variant of this argument see Ellen Meiksins Wood, 'Class, race, and capitalism', in Diane E. David (ed.), *Political Power and Social Theory*, Emerald, London, 2002.

24 Mirna Safi, *Les Inégalités ethno-raciales*, La Découverte, Paris, 2013, ch. 3.

25 See Neil Chakraborti and Jon Garland (eds.), *Rural Racism*, London: Routledge, 2012. On this question see also Raymond Williams, *The Country and the City*, Oxford University Press, Oxford, 1975.

26 Robert D. Bullard et al., *Toxic Waste and Race at Twenty, 1987–2007*, op. cit., p. 109.

27 See their website at www.ben-network.co.uk.

28 See Guillaume Faburel et Sandrine Gueymard, 'Inégalités environnementales en région Île-de-France: le rôle structurant des facteurs négatifs de l'environnement et des choix politiques afférents', *Espaces, populations, sociétés*, 1, 2008.

29 Ibid., p. 165.

30 [Urban areas identified by the French state as particular centres of social problems.]

31 For an overall view of the spatial dimension of ethno-racial inequalities in France, see Mirna Safi, *Les Inégalités ethno-raciales*, op. cit., ch. 4.

32 Anne-Jeanne Naudé, 'Le saturnisme, une maladie sociale de l'immigration', *Hommes et migrations*, 1225, May–June 2000, p. 13. See also *Bulletin épidémiologique hebdomadaire*, 13 January 1992.

33 Pascale Dietrich-Ragon, 'Le logement insalubre', *Esprit*, January 2012, p. 67. For a social history of slums in France, see Roger-Henri Guerrand, 'Histoire des taudis', in Serge Paugam (ed.), *L'Exclusion, l'état des savoirs*, La Découverte, Paris, 1996.

34 Anne-Jeanne Naudé, 'Le saturnisme, une maladie sociale de l'immigration', loc. cit., p. 17. On the US case, see also Helen Epstein, 'Lead poisoning. The ignored scandal', *New York Review of Books*, 21 March 2013.

35 Institut français de l'environnement (IFEN), *Les Synthèses*, 2006 issue, available at http://www.statistiques.developpement-durable.gouv.fr/fileadmin/documents/Themes/Environnement/ree/2006/18-inegalites-environnementales-ree-2006.pdf.

36 Ibid., p. 423. See also Gwénael Letombe et Bernard Zuindeau, 'Gestion des externalités environnementales dans le bassin minier du Nord-Pas-de-Calais: une approche en termes de proximité', *Développement durable et territoire*, 7, 2006.

37 Available at http://www.washingtonpost.com/wp-dyn/content/article/2007/06/15/AR2007061501857.html.

38 See its website at www.savedarfur.org/.

39 See Alex de Waal, 'Counter-insurgency on the cheap', *London Review of Books*, 26 (15), August 2004.

40 See Mahmood Mamdani, *Saviours and Survivors. Darfur, Politics, and the War on Terror*, Verso, London, 2008.

41 See Florence Brisset-Foucault, 'Darfour, généalogies d'un conflit. Entretien avec Jérôme Tubiana', *Mouvements*, November 2007.

42 Younes Abouyoub, 'Climate: the forgotten culprit. The ecological dimension of the Darfur conflict', *Race, Gender, and Class*, 19 (1–2), 2012, p. 161.

43 Ibid., p. 164.

44 Alex de Waal, 'Counter-insurgency on the cheap', cit.

45 See Florence Brisset-Foucault, 'Darfour, généalogies d'un conflit. Entretien avec Jérôme Tubiana', loc. cit.

46 Younes Abouyoub, 'Climate: the forgotten culprit. The ecological dimension of the Darfur conflict', loc. cit., p. 170.

47 Ibid., p. 153.

48 Welzer, *Climate Wars*, op. cit., p. 103.

49 Henri Lefebvre, *The Production of Space*, Oxford University Press, Oxford, 1991.

50 Razmig Keucheyan, *Le Constructivisme. Des origines à nos jours*, Hermann, Paris, 2007.

51 See for example Bruno Latour's *Politics of Nature: How to Bring the Sciences into Democracy*, Harvard University Press, Cambridge, MA, 2004.

52 For definitions that partly corroborate our own, see Marianne Chaumel and Stéphane La Branche, 'Inégalités écologiques: vers quelle définition?', loc. cit.; Cyria Emelianoff, 'La problématique des inégalités écologiques, un nouveau paysage conceptuel', *Écologie & politique*, 35 (1), 2008; Andrew Szase and Michael Meuser, 'Environmental inequalities. Literature review and proposals for new directions in research and theory', *Current Sociology*, 45, 1997.

53 See Wanda Diebolt et al., 'Les inégalités écologiques en milieu urbain', *Rapport de l'inspection générale de l'Environnement*, Ministère de l'Écologie et du Développement durable, April 2005, p. 13. Available at: www.ladocumentationfrancaise.fr/var/storage/rapports-publics/054000572/0000.pdf.

54 Ibid., p. 1.

55 See Kenneth A. Gould et Tammy L. Lewis (eds.), *Twenty Lessons in Environmental Sociology*, op. cit., p. 249–250.

56 Wanda Diebolt et al., 'Les inégalités écologiques en milieu urbain', loc. cit., p. 52.

57 Institut français de l'environnement (IFEN), *Les Synthèses*, op. cit. p. 420.

58 Ibid., p. 422.

59 See the communiqué by the UFC-Que choisir, from 20 March 2012: www.quechoisir.org/environnement-energie/eau/eau-potable/communique-qualite-de-l-eau-du-robinet-en-france-l-appel-e-au-secours-de-l-ufc-que-choisir.

60 See Lionel Charles et al., 'Les multiples facettes des inégalités écologiques', *Développement durable et territoires*, 9, 2007, p. 8.

61 *Le Monde*, 19 November 2012.

62 *Le Monde*, 2 February 2012.

63 *Le Monde*, 13 March 2013.

64 See Michel Kokoreff and Didier Lapeyrnnie, *Refaire la cité. L'avenir des banlieues*, Le Seuil, Paris, 2013, pp. 97–98.

65 Wanda Diebolt et al., 'Les inégalités écologiques en milieu urbain', loc. cit., p. 17.

66 Marianne Chaumel and Stéphane la Branche, 'Inégalités écologiques : vers quelle définition?', loc. cit., p. 104.

67 Report by the Institut national de veille sanitaire (INVS), July 2004, p. 48. Available at http://www.invs.sante.fr/publications/2004/chaleur2003_170904/rapport_canicule.pdf.

68 Éloi Laurent, 'Écologie et inégalités', loc. cit., p. 52. On this question, see also Alain Lipietz, 'Économie politique des écotaxes' *Rapports du Conseil d'analyse économique*, 8, La Documentation française, April 1998.

69 Salvador Juan, 'L'inégalité écologique, une notion écran', *Écologie & politique*, 45 (1), 2012, p. 152.

70 See Stéphane Latté's dissertation, *Les Victimes. La formation d'une catégorie sociale improbable et ses usages dans l'action collective*, École normale supérieure, Paris, 2008. HLMs are rent-controlled or social housing.

71 Ibid.

72 On the working-class neighbourhoods of Toulouse, see Michel Kokoreff and Didier Lapeyronnie, *Refaire la cité. L'avenir des banlieues*, op. cit., ch. 2.

73 *Le Monde*, 19 December 2012.

74 'Poverty of philosophy', in *Marx-Engels Collected Works*, Vol. 6, Lawrence & Wishart, London, 1976, p. 167.

75 See Mark Fiege, *The Republic of Nature. An Environmental History of the United States*, University of Washington Press, Seattle, 2012, ch. 3.

76 Ibid., p. 103.

77 Ibid., p. 119.

78 Ibid., p. 122.

79 Elizabeth D. Blum, 'Power, danger, and control. Slave women's perception of wilderness in the nineteenth century', *Women's Studies*, 31 (2), January 2002, pp. 247–265.

80 See Merrill Singer, 'Down cancer alley. The lived experience of health and environmental suffering in Louisiana's chemical corridor', *Medical Anthropology Quarterly*, 25 (2), 2011.

81 *Le Monde*, 9 February 2013.

82 Valerie L. Kuletz, *Tainted Desert. Environmental Ruin in the American West*, Routledge, New York, 1998.

83 Gregory Hooks and Chad Smith, 'The treadmill of destruction. National sacrifice areas and Native Americans', *American Sociological Review*, 69 (4), 2004.

84 Daniel Bensaïd, *Les Dépossédés. Marx, les voleurs de bois et le droit des pauvres*, La Fabrique, Paris, 2007. See also Edward P. Thompson, *Whigs and Hunters. The Origin of the Black Act*, Pantheon Books, London, 1975.

85 Caroline Ford, 'Nature, culture, and conservation in France and her colonies, 1840–1940', *Past and Present*, 183, May 2004, p. 180.

86 Ibid., p. 181.

87 Fabien Locher and Jean-Baptiste Fressoz, 'Modernity's frail climate. A climate history of environmental reflexivity', *Critical Inquiry*, 38 (3), Spring 2012.

88 Yann Drouet and Antoine Luciani, 'À l'origine du ski français. Le discours commun de l'armée et du Club alpin français (1902–1907)', *Staps*, 71 (1), 2006.

89 William Cronon, 'The trouble with wilderness; or, getting back to the wrong nature', *in* William Cronon (ed.), *Uncommon Ground. Rethinking the Human Place in Nature*, op. cit.

90 See Theodor Adorno, 'On Lyric Poetry and Society', in *Notes to Literature*, Vol. I, Columbia University Press, New York, 1991. Hartmut Stenzel, 'Évolution et fonction critique du concept de nature dans la littérature romantique et dans le socialisme utopique', *Romantisme*, 30, 1980.

91 Adam Rome, '"Give earth a chance". The environmental movement and the sixties', *Journal of American History*, September 2003.

92 Hartmut Rosa, *Accélération. Une critique sociale du temps*, La Découverte, Paris, 2010.

93 John K. Galbraith, *The Affluent Society*, Harcourt, New York, 1998. On this point, see also Ramachandra Guha, 'Radical American environmentalism and wilderness preservation. A third world critique', *Environmental Ethics*, 11, 1989, p. 7.

94 Quoted in Eileen Maura McGurty, 'From NIMBY to civil rights. The origins of the environmental justice movement', loc. cit., p. 305.

95 See Carolyn Merchant, 'Shades of darkness. Race and environmental history', *Environmental History*, 8 (3), 2003. See also (by the same author) *The Death of Nature. Women, Ecology, and The Scientific Revolution*, Harper, New York, 1990.

96 Mark Fiege, *The Republic of Nature. An Environmental History of the United States*, op. cit., ch. 8.

97 See Mike Davis, *Planet of Slums*, Verso, London, 2007.

98 On the analogies between individuals' character and the environment within which they are active, as according to nineteenth-century literature and particularly Balzac, see Franco Moretti, *The Bourgeois. Between History and Literature*, Verso, London, 2013, p. 92.

99 In this regard see Maxime Cervulle, 'L'identité blanche et sa critique. Les *critical white studies* en débat', in Maxime Quijoux et al., *Cultures et inégalités. Enquête sur les dimensions culturelles des rapports sociaux*, L'Harmattan, Paris, 2011.

100 See Jean Starobinski, *Jean-Jacques Rousseau : la transparence et l'obstacle*, Gallimard, Paris, 1976, ch. 2.

101 Carolyn Merchant, 'Shades of darkness. Race and environmental history', loc. cit., p. 380.

102 Elsa Dorlin, *La Matrice de la race. Généalogie sexuelle et coloniale de la Nation française*, La Découverte, Paris, 2009.

103 [*Matrice* can mean either womb or matrix.]

104 Ramachandra Guha, 'Radical American environmentalism and wilderness preservation. A third world critique', loc. cit., p. 2. On the history of national parks in France, see Adel Selmi, 'L'émergence de l'idée de parc national en France. De la protection des paysages à l'expérimentation coloniale', *in* Raphaël Larrère et al., *Histoire des parcs nationaux. Comment prendre soin de la nature ?*, Éditions Quæ, Paris, 2009; Florian Charvolin, 'L'affaire de la Vanoise et son analyste. Le document, le bouquetin et le parc national', *Vingtième siècle*, 11 (2), 2012.

105 For a *longue-durée* conception of ecological imperialism, see Alfred W. Crosby, *Ecological Imperialism. The Biological Expansion of Europe, 900–1900*, Cambridge University Press, Cambridge, 2004.

106 Reuben Matheka, 'The international dimension of the politics of wild-life conservation in Kenya, 1958–1968', *Journal of Eastern African Studies*, 2 (1), 2008.

107 Linda Steet, *Veils and Daggers. A Century of National Geographic's Representation of the Arab World*, Temple University Press, Philadelphia, 2000.

108 Richard H. Grove, *Green Imperialism. Colonial Expansion, Tropical Island, and the Origins of Environmentalism, 1600–1860*, Cambridge University Press, Cambridge, 1996; Thomas Robertson, 'This is the American earth. American empire, the cold war, and American environmentalism', *Diplomatic History*, 32 (4), September 2008.

109 On this see Yannick Mahrane et al., 'De la nature à la biosphère. L'invention politique de l'environnement global, 1945–1972', *Vingtième siècle*, 113 (1), 2012.

110 See Fabien Locher, 'Les pâturages de la guerre froide : Garrett Hardin et la "Tragédie des communs"', *Revue d'histoire moderne et contemporaine*, 60–61 (1), 2013, pp. 32 et seq.

111 Patrick Chaskiel, 'Syndicalisme et risque industriel. Avant et après la catastrophe de l'usine AZF de Toulouse (septembre 2001)', *Sociologie du travail*, 49, 2007, p. 182.

112 See *Lutte ouvrière*, 1757, 29 March 2002.

113 Danielle Tartakowsky, 'La CGT, du hors-travail au "cadre de vie"', *in* Joël Hedde (ed.), *La CGT de 1966 à 1984: l'empreinte de mai 1968*, Institut CGT d'histoire sociale, Montreuil, 2009.

114 Renaud Bécot, 'L'invention syndicale de l'environnement dans la France des années 1960', *Vingtième siècle*, 113 (1), 2012, p. 171.

115 Darryn Snell and Peter Fairbrother, 'Unions as environmental actors', *Transfer. European Review of Labour and Research*, 16, 2010.

116 Patrick Chaskiel, 'Syndicalisme et risque industriel. Avant et après la catastrophe de l'usine AZF de Toulouse (septembre 2001)', loc. cit., p. 184.

117 In this regard see Guillaume Faburel and Isabelle Maleyre, 'Le bruit des avions comme facteur de dépréciations immobilières, de polarisation sociale et d'inégalités environnementales. Le cas d'Orly', *Développement durable et territoire*, 9, 2007.

118 Renaud Bécot, 'L'invention syndicale de l'environnement dans la France des années 1960', loc. cit., p. 174. In the 1970s, the CFDT union confederation also devoted itself to the anti-nuclear movement, for which it produced a 'counter-expertise'. On this topic see Sezin Topçu, 'Critique du nucléaire et gouvernement de l'opinion', interview with Fabien Locher, *Contretemps*, 13 July 2011.

119 Danielle Tartakowsky, 'La CGT, du hors-travail au "cadre de vie"', loc. cit.

120 [An alliance of the Socialists, Communists and other smaller left-wing parties.]

121 Michel Dobry, *Sociologie des crises politiques. La dynamique des mobilisations multisectorielles*, Presses de Sciences Po, Paris, 1992.

122 Renaud Bécot, 'L'invention syndicale de l'environnement dans la France des années 1960', loc. cit., p. 172.

123 Sophie Béroud, 'Les opérations "Robin des Bois" au sein de la CGT Énergie. Quand la cause des chômeurs et des "sans" contribue à la redéfinition de l'action syndicale', *Revue française de science politique*, 59 (1), 2009.

124 See Eric Hobsbawm, *Bandits*, The New Press, New York, 2000.

125 Sophie Béroud, 'Les opérations "Robin des Bois" au sein de la CGT Énergie. Quand la cause des chômeurs et des "sans" contribue à la redéfinition de l'action syndicale', loc. cit., p. 108.

2 Financializing Nature: Insuring Climatic Risks

1 Ian Baucum, *Specters of the Atlantic. Finance Capital, Slavery, and the Philosophy of History*, Duke University Press, Durham 2005, ch. 3.

2 Giovanni Arrighi, *The Long Twentieth Century*, op. cit.

3 On the ideology of 'adventure' accompanying the risk inherent to the global expansion of capitalism in the seventeenth and eighteenth centuries, see Franco Moretti, *The Bourgeois*, op. cit., ch. 1. Daniel Defoe's *Robinson Crusoe* (1719) was one of the first literary incarnations of this ideology.

4 Ian Baucom, *Specters of the Atlantic*, op. cit., p. 104.

5 Olivier Godard et al., *Traité des nouveaux risques*, Gallimard, Paris, 2002, p. 363.

6 See Peter Borscheid (ed.), *World Insurance. The Evolution of a Global Risk Network*, Oxford University Press, Oxford, 2012.

7 P. G. M. Dickson, *The Financial Revolution in England. A Study of the Development of Public Credit, 1688–1756*, MacMillan, London, 1967.

8 Ian Baucom, *Specters of the Atlantic*, op. cit., p. 96.

9 See François Ewald, 'L'assurantialisation de la société française', *Les Tribunes de la santé*, 31 (2), 2011.

10 In this regard see Viviana Zelizer, *Morals and Markets. The Development of Life Insurance in the United States*, Columbia University Press, New York, 1979.

11 [The French adjective used here, 'branché', also has the sense of 'trendy'.]

12 Analysis of the causes of the crisis is, of course, a matter of controversy among critical economists. Our approach here is inspired by the perspective elaborated by Robert Brenner in his *The Economics of Global Turbulence*, Verso, London, 2006. For a different point of view, see Leo Panitch and Sam Gindin, *The Making of Global Capitalism. The Political Economy of American Empire*, Verso, London, 2012.

13 See, for example, Fredric Jameson, 'The politics of utopia', *New Left Review*, 25, January–February 2004. See also Peter Fitting, 'The concept of utopia in the work of Fredric Jameson', *Utopian Studies*, 9 (2), 1998.

14 Frédéric Morlaye, *Risk management et assurance*, Economica, Paris, 2006, p. 10–12. See also École nationale d'assurance de Paris, *Manuel international de l'assurance*, Economica, Paris, 2005.

15 Olivier Godard et al., *Traité des nouveaux risques*, op. cit., p. 381.

16 Arthur Charpentier, 'Insurability of climate risks', *Geneva Papers*, International Association for the Study of Insurance Economics, 33, 2008.

17 Frank H. Knight, *Risk, Uncertainty, and Profit*, Dover, New York, 2006 (first edition: 1921).

18 Philip D. Bougen, 'Catastrophe risk', *Economy and Society* 32 (2), 2003, p. 258.

19 Frédéric Morlaye, *Risk management et assurance*, op. cit., p. 16.

20 For an interesting reflection on this theme, See Dean Curran, 'Risk society and the distribution of bads. Theorizing class in the risk society', *The British Journal of Sociology*, 64 (1), 2013.

21 Grégory Quenet, 'La catastrophe, un objet historique?', *Hypothèses*, 1, 1999; Jean-Pierre Dupuy, *Pour un catastrophisme éclairé. Quand l'impossible est certain*, Le Seuil, Paris, 2004. In the final decades of the twentieth century, disaster studies became a whole separate research field in the social sciences. In this regard, see Sandrine Revet 'Penser et affronter les désastres: un panorama des recherches en sciences sociales et des politiques internationales', *Critique internationale*, 52 (3), 2011.

22 David M. Cutler and Richard J. Zeckhauser, 'Reinsurance for catastrophes and cataclysms', National Bureau of Economics Research, Working paper no. 5913, 1997.

23 www.swissre.com/sigma/ and, more particularly, 'Natural Catastrophes and Man-Made disasters in 2011', *Sigma*, 2, 2012. The following data are from that issue.

24 Koko Warner et al., 'Adaptation to climate change. Linking disaster risk reduction and insurance', United Nations International Strategy for Disaster Reduction Secretariat (UNISDR), 2009, p. 4. Available at www.preventionweb.net/files/9654_linkingdrrinsurance .pdf. The reinsurer Munich Re and the World Bank took an active part in producing this document, issued by the United Nations.

25 On this see William S. Milberg, 'Shifting sources and uses of profit. Sustaining US financialization with global value chains', *Economy and Society*, 37 (3), 2008.

26 Mike Davis, *Planet of Slums*, op. cit.

27 Michael Lewis, 'In nature's casino', *New York Times*, 26 August 2007.

28 Arthur Charpentier, 'Insurability of climate risks', loc. cit., p. 103.

29 See the data available on the website of the Fédération française des sociétés d'assurance (FFSA), for instance www.ffsa.fr/sites/ jcms/fn_53027/catastrophes-naturelles-l-inondation-reste-e-risque -n1-en-france?cc=fn_7360.

30 For example in Immanuel Wallerstein, *World-Systems Analysis*, Duke University Press, Durham, NC, 2004.

31 Jason Moore, 'Cheap food and bad money. Food, frontiers, and financialization in the rise and demise of neoliberalism', *Review. A Journal of the Fernand Braudel Center*, 33, 2012.

32 Richard V. Ericson and Aaron Doyle, 'Catastrophe risk, insurance, and terrorism', *Economy and Society*, 33 (2), 2004, p. 157.

33 Frédéric Morlaye, *Risk Management et assurance*, op. cit., p. 128.

34 Olivier Godard et al., *Traité des nouveaux risques*, op. cit., p. 368; Geoffrey Heal and Howard Kunreuther, 'Modeling interdependent risk', *Risk Analysis*, 27 (3), 2007.

35 Ulrich Beck, *Risk Society: Toward a New Modernity*, Sage, London, 1992. For a critique of this theory, see Dean Curran, 'Risk society and the distribution of bads. Theorizing class in the risk society', loc. cit.

36 See Anthony Giddens, *Beyond Left and Right. The Future of Radical Politics*, Polity, London, 1994.

37 Ulrich Beck, *The cosmopolitan vision*, Cambridge, Polity, 2006. See also Ulrich Beck, 'The terrorist threat. World risk society revisited', *Theory, Culture, and Society*, 19, 2002.

38 Bernard Durant, 'L'assurance du risque nucléaire', *Mines-Énergie*, 402, January–February 2003.

39 See its website at www.assuratome.fr/.

40 See the figures available on the *L'Argus de l'Assurance* site at www.argusdelassurance.com/acteurs/fukushima-un-an-apres.54827.

41 [A business association and lobby group similar to Britain's CBI.]

42 On François Ewald's trajectory and his relations with Foucault, see Michael C. Behrent, 'Accidents happen. François Ewald, the "antirevolutionary" Foucault, and the intellectual politics of the French welfare state', *Journal of Modern History*, 82, September 2010.

43 François Ewald and Denis Kessler, 'Les noces du risque et de la politique', *Le Débat*, 109 (2), 2000.

44 Michael C. Behrent, 'Accidents happen. François Ewald, the "antirevolutionary" Foucault, and the intellectual politics of the French welfare state', loc. cit., p. 622.

45 François Ewald, 'La véritable nature du risque de développement et sa garantie', *Risques*, 14, April 1993.

46 Richard V. Ericson and Aaron Doyle, 'Catastrophe risk, insurance, and terrorism', loc. cit., p. 155.

47 Frédéric Morlaye, *Risk management et assurance*, op. cit., p. 26.

48 Jean-Baptiste Fressoz, *L'Apocalypse joyeuse. Une histoire du risque technologique*, Le Seuil, Paris, 2012.

49 An early version of this argument appears in his 1968 work 'Technology and Science as Ideology', which appears in English in his *Toward a Rational Society: Student Protest, Science, and Politics*, Beacon Press, Boston, 1970.

50 Richard V. Ericson and Aaron Doyle, 'Catastrophe risk, insurance, and terrorism', loc. cit., p. 142.

51 OCDE, 'Terrorism risk insurance in OECD countries', *Policy Issues in Insurance*, 9, 2005.

52 Tony Norfield, 'Derivatives and capitalist markets. The speculative heart of capital', *Historical Materialism*, 20 (1), 2012.

53 See, on this, www.artemis.bm/blog/2009/04/28/a-swine-flu-pandemic-and-the-catastrophe-bond-market/.

54 Erwann Michel-Kerjan et al., 'Catastrophe financing for governments. Learning from the 2009–2012 multicat program in Mexico', *OECD Working Papers on Finance, Insurance and Private Pensions*, 9, 2011, p. 17.

55 There is a description of this practice in Michael Lewis, 'In nature's casino', loc. cit.

56 Frédéric Morlaye, *Risk management et assurance*, op. cit., p. 149.

57 Erwann Michel-Kerjan et al., 'Catastrophe financing for governments. Learning from the 2009–2012 multicat program in Mexico', loc. cit., p. 14.

58 See www.artemis.bm/deal_directory/.

59 Frédéric Morlaye, *Risk management et assurance*, op. cit., p. 147.

60 See the figures available at www.risk.net/insurance-risk/news/2132528/sovereign-debt-crisis-spurs-investment-cat-bonds.

61 See the sites www.air-worldwide.com/Home/AIR-Worldwide/, www.eqe-cat.com/ and www.rms.com/.

62 Melinda Cooper, 'Turbulent worlds. Financial markets and environmental crisis', *Theory, Culture, and Society*, 27, 2010.

63 Michael Lewis, 'In nature's casino', loc. cit.

64 A nephila is a type of spider able to foresee bad weather, which spins its web higher when the weather is good and lower down when bad weather is coming.

65 Philip D. Bougen, 'Catastrophe risk', loc. cit., p. 265.

66 Richard V. Ericson and Aaron Doyle, 'Catastrophe risk, insurance, and terrorism', loc. cit., p. 148.

67 Ibid., p. 149.

68 Philip D. Bougen, 'Catastrophe risk', loc. cit., p. 267.

69 Karl Marx, *Grundrisse*, ch. 3, available online at https://www.marxists.org/archive/marx/works/1857/grundrisse/ch03.htm.

70 Alfred Sohn-Rethel, *Intellectual and Manual Labour*, Humanities Press, Atlantic Highlands, 1978. Alberto Toscano, 'The open secret of real abstractions', *Rethinking Marxism*, 20 (2), 2008.

71 See Moishe Postone, *Time, Labor and Social Domination: A Reinterpretation of Marx's Critical Theory*, Cambridge University Press, Cambridge, 1993. On the problem of fixing prices for natural entities, see also Marion Fourcade, 'Price and prejudice. On economics and the enchantment (and disenchantment) of nature', *in* Jens Beckert and Patrik Aspers (eds.), *The Worth of Goods*, Oxford University Press, Oxford, 2010.

72 Larry Lohmann, 'Uncertainty markets and carbon markets. Variations on polanyian themes', *New Political Economy*, 15 (2), 2010, p. 232.

73 Donald MacKenzie, 'Is economics performative? Option theory and the construction of derivatives markets', *Journal of the History of Economic Thought*, 28, 2006; 'The credit crisis as a problem in the sociology of knowledge', *American Journal of Sociology*, 116, 2011.

74 Bram Büshcher, 'Derivative nature. Interrogating the value of conservation in boundless Southern Africa', *Third World Quarterly*, 31 (2), 2010.

75 Peter Newell and Matthew Paterson, *Climate Capitalism. Global Warming and the Transformation of the Global Economy*, Cambridge University Press, Cambridge, 2010.

76 Robert Fletcher, 'Capitalizing on chaos. Climate change and disaster capitalism', *Ephemera*, 12 (1/2), 2012, p. 103.

77 See Peter Newell and Matthew Paterson, *Climate Capitalism*, op. cit., p. 89.

78 Larry Lohmann, 'Uncertainty markets and carbon markets. Variations on polanyian themes', loc. cit., p. 243. See also Steffen Böhm et al., 'Greening capitalism? A Marxist critique of carbon markets', *Organization Studies*, 33 (11), 2012.

79 Kate Ervine, 'Carbon markets, debt and uneven development', *Third World Quarterly*, 34 (4), 2013.

80 Koko Warner et al., 'Adaptation to climate change. Linking disaster risk reduction and insurance', op. cit., p. 4.

81 Wendy J. Werner, 'Micro-insurance in Bangladesh. Risk protection for the poor?', *Journal of Health, Population, and Nutrition*, 27 (4), 2007.

82 Randy Martin, *The Financialization of Daily Life*, Temple University Press, Philadelphia, 2002.

83 See the two thick volumes jointly published by Munich Re and the ILO in 2006, entitled *Protecting the Poor. A Micro-insurance Compendium*, available at www.munichre-foundation.org/home/Microinsurance/MicroinsuranceCompendium.html. In it we can

read, for example, the contribution by Thomas Loster and Dirk Reinhardt, 'Micro-insurance and climate change'.

84 David Harvey, *The New Imperialism*, Oxford University Press, Oxford, 2010. See also Larry Lohmann, 'Financialization, commodification and carbon. The contradictions of neoliberal climate policy', *Socialist Register*, 48, 2012.

85 Michèle Laubscher, 'Modèles de marché pour les pauvres', *Global. Globalisation et politique Nord-Sud*, 40, Summer 2011.

86 See the Swiss Re document 'Closing the financial gap. New partnerships between the public and the private sectors to finance disaster risks', 2011, available online at: http://media.swissre.com/documents/pub_closing_the_financial_gap_W1.pdf.

87 Michèle Laubscher, 'Modèles de marché pour les pauvres', loc. cit.

88 ['Helvétique' is an archaic/literary way of saying 'Swiss', based on the Latin world 'helvetica'.]

89 *Neue Zürcher Zeitung*, 21 July 2010.

90 David Croson and David Richter, 'Sovereign cat bonds and infrastructure project financing', *Risk Analysis*, 23 (3), 2003.

91 See the website at www.unisdr.org/.

92 See the Center's website at www.wharton.upenn.edu/risk-center/.

93 Erwann Michel-Kerjan et al., 'Catastrophe financing for governments. Learning from the 2009–2012 multicat program in Mexico', loc. cit., p. 25.

94 Ibid., p. 24.

95 Ibid., p. 36.

96 Arthur Charpentier, 'Insurability of climate risks', loc. cit., p. 100.

97 ASEAN, 'Advancing disaster risk financing and insurance in ASEAN countries. Framework and options for implementation', April 2012. Available online at: www.gfdrr.org/sites/gfdrr.org/files/publication/DRFI_ASEAN_REPORT_June12.pdf.

98 Swiss Re, 'Insurance in the emerging markets: overview and prospects for Islamic insurance', 5, 2008. Available online at http://media.swis-sre.com/documents/sigma5_2008_en.pdf.

99 World Bank, *Debt Servicing Handbook*, June 2009, p. 16, available online at http://siteresources.worldbank.org/PROJECTS/Resources/40940-1250176637898/Engl.pdf.

100 Ibid., pp. 19–20.

101 Erwann Michel-Kerjan et al., 'Catastrophe financing for governments. Learning from the 2009–2012 multicat program in Mexico', loc. cit., p. 3.

102 Costas Lapavitsas, 'Financialised capitalism. Crisis and financial expropriation', *Historical Materialism*, 17 (2), 2009.

103 Arthur Charpentier, 'Insurability of climate risks', loc. cit., p. 91.
104 Frédéric Morlaye, *Risk Management et assurance*, op. cit., p. 173.
105 Melinda Cooper, 'Turbulent worlds. Financial markets and environmental crisis', loc. cit., p. 177.
106 John E. Thornes, 'An introduction to weather and climate derivatives', *Weather*, 58, May 2003; Samuel Randalls, 'Weather profits. Weather derivatives and the commercialization of meteorology', *Social Studies of Science*, 40, 2010; Michael Pryke, 'Geomoney. An option on frost, going long on clouds', *Geoforum*, 38, 2007.
107 See John E. Thornes and Samuel Randalls, 'Commodifying the atmosphere. Pennies from heaven?', *Geografiska Annaler*, 89 (4), 2007.
108 Donald MacKenzie and Yuval Millo, 'Constructing a market, performing a theory. The historical sociology of a financial derivatives exchange', *American Journal of Sociology*, 109 (1), 2003.
109 Leo Panitch and Sam Gindin, *The Making of Global Capitalism*, op. cit., pp. 140–150.
110 James T. Mandel, C. Josh Donlan and Jonathan Armstrong, 'A derivative approach to endangered species conservation', *Frontiers in Ecology and the Environment*, 8, 2010.
111 Hélène Tordjman and Valérie Boisvert, 'L'idéologie marchande au service de la biodiversité?', *Mouvements*, 70, 2012, p. 36.
112 Timothy Mitchell, *Carbon democracy. Political Power in the Age of Oil*, Verso, London, 2011.
113 James O'Connor, *Natural Causes*, op. cit.
114 Neil Smith, 'Nature as accumulation strategy', *Socialist Register*, 43, 2007.
115 Robert Fletcher, 'Capitalizing on chaos. Climate change and disaster capitalism', loc. cit.

3 Green Wars, or the Militarization of Ecology

1 *National Security Strategy*, May 2010, available on the White House site at: www.whitehouse.gov/sites/default/files/rss_viewer/national_security_strategy.pdf.
2 See Kurt M. Campbell et al., 'The age of consequences. The foreign policy and national security implications of global climate change', Center for Strategic and International Studies and Center for a New American Security, November 2007, p. 5. Available at: http://csis.org/files/media/csis/pubs/071105_ageofconsequences.pdf.

3 See 'National security and the threat of climate change', Center for Naval Analysis, 2007, p. 35. Available online at: www.cna.org/cna_files/pdf/national%20security%20and%20the%20threat%20of%20climate%20change.pdf. On the geopolitical implications of rising sea levels, see Henrike Brecht et al., 'Sea-level rise and storm surges. High stakes for a small number of developing countries', *Journal of Environment & Development*, 21 (1), 2012.

4 François Gemenne, *Géopolitique du changement climatique*, op. cit., p. 8.

5 Thomas Schelling, 'Some economics of global warming', *The American Economic Review*, 82 (1), March 1992. See also the interview with Schelling in *The Atlantic*, July 2009.

6 Dominique Bourg and Gérald Hess, 'La géo-ingénierie: réduction, adaptation et scénario du désespoir', *Natures Sciences Sociétés*, 18, 2010.

7 Ronald E. Doel, 'Quelle place pour les sciences de l'environnement physique dans l'histoire environnementale?' *Revue d'histoire moderne et contemporaine*, 56 (4), 2009, p. 142.

8 Peter Coates et al., 'Defending nation, defending nature? Militarized landscapes and military environmentalism in Britain, France, and the United States', *Environmental History*, 16, July 2011, p. 469. In this same perspective, see also Chris Pearson, 'Researching military landscapes. A literature review on war and the militarization of the environment', *Landscape Research*, 37 (1), 2012.

9 See Anders Fogh Rasmussen's column, 'NATO and climate change', 15 December 2009, *Huffington Post*. Available at: www.huffington-post.com/anders-fogh-rasmussen/nato-and-climate-change_b_392409.html.

10 [Leading member of France's *Parti Socialiste* and a former prime minister.]

11 See *Rapport d'information sur l'impact du changement climatique en matière de sécurité et de défense*, présenté par André Schneider and Philippe Tourtelier, Assemblée nationale, commission des Affaires européennes, 28 February 2012. Available online at: www.assemblee-nationale.fr/13/europe/rap-info/i4415.asp.

12 [The *Union pour un Mouvement Populaire* was the main party of the centre-right at the time and the *Parti Socialiste* the main party of the centre-left.]

13 See *Le Monde*, 15 March 2012.

14 See Geoffrey D. Dabelko, 'Planning for climate change. The security community's precautionary principle', *Climatic Change*, 96, 2009, p. 13.

15 On this question, see http://ecologie.blog.lemonde.fr/2011/07/22/bientot-des-casques-verts-du-changement-climatique-a-lonu/.

16 A version of this argument is advanced by Dominique Bourg and Kerry Whiteside in *Vers une démocratie écologique le citoyen, le savant et le politique*, Le Seuil, Paris, 2010.

17 Karl von Clausewitz, *On War*, text taken from https://www.marxists.org/reference/archive/clausewitz/works/on-war/book2/ch02.htm.

18 Nicos Poulantzas, *State, Power, Socialism*, Verso, London, 2000, p. 127.

19 Hans Jonas, 'Zur ontologischen grundlegung einer zukunftsethik', in *Philosophische Untersuchungen und metaphysische Vermutungen*, Insel Verlag, Frankfurt am Main, 1992.

20 Ibid.

21 Paul Kennedy, *The Rise and Fall of the Great Powers*, Vintage, London, 1989.

22 On this, see www.spiegel.de/international/europe/the-greek-military-budget-offers-plenty-of-room-for-cuts-a-846607.html. On the link between the US armed forces and the fiscal crisis, see Mark D. Troutman, 'Fiscal jeopardy. The strategic risks of US debt and how to avoid them', *Armed Forces Journal*, February 2011.

23 See John Mearsheimer, *The Tragedy of Great Power Politics*, WW Norton, New York, 2002.

24 Hervé Kempf, *Comment les riches détruisent la planète*, Points, Paris, 2009, p. 27.

25 See Kenneth Pomeranz, 'The great Himalayan watershed', *New Left Review*, 58, July–August 2009.

26 *Le Monde*, 12 March 2012.

27 Mike Davis, *Planet of Slums*, op. cit.

28 See Jean-Louis Dufour, *La Guerre, la Ville et le Soldat*, Odile Jacob, Paris, 2002 and also his 'L'armée face à la ville', *Annales de la recherche urbaine*, 91, 2001.

29 See the *Failed States Index* published by *Foreign Policy* online at www.foreign-policy.com/failedstates.

30 See www.foreignpolicy.com/articles/2011/06/20/postcards_from _hell_2011#14.

31 Robert D. Kaplan, 'The coming anarchy', *The Atlantic*, February 1994. John Mearsheimer advances a similar point of view on the 'imbalances' resulting from the end of the Cold War in his 'Back to the future. Instability in Europe after the cold war', *International Security*, 15 (1), 1990.

32 Noam Chomsky, *The New Military Humanism*, Pluto Press, London, 1999.

33 See, in this regard, *The Economist*, 10 April 2008, as well as Michael Baker, 'The coming conflicts of climate change', *Council on Foreign Relations*, 7 September 2010. On the implications that climate change has for Africa, see Oli Brown et al., 'Climate change

as the new security threat. Implications for Africa', *International Affairs*, 83 (6), 2007.

34 See *Le Monde*, 14–15 October 2012.

35 Thomas Robertson, 'This is the American earth. American empire, the cold war, and American environmentalism', loc. cit.

36 See Gregory J. Parker, 'The future of seabasing', *Armed Forces Journal*, December 2010.

37 See   www.undg.org/archive_docs/7339-Afghanistan__Green _Afghanistan_Initiative__GAIN_.pdf.

38 Christian Parenti, *Tropic of Chaos. Climate Change and the New Geography of Violence*, Nation Books, New York, 2012, pp. 106–107.

39 Ibid., p. 107.

40 See Christine Parthemore and Will Rogers, 'Sustaining security. How natural resources influence national security', Center for a New American Security, June 2010, p. 8. Available online at: www.cnas.org/files/documents/publications/CNAS_Sustaining%20 Security_Parthemore%20Rogers.pdf.

41 Hervé de Courrèges et al., *Principes de contre-insurrection*, Economica, Paris, 2010, p. 69.

42 Ibid., p. 72.

43 Daniel Süri, 'Les naxalites : la plus grande des guérillas dans la plus grande des démocratie', *Revue des livres*, February 2012; Joël Cabalion, 'Maoïsme et lutte armée en Inde contemporaine', *La Vie des idées*, 9 March 2011.

44 David Harvey, *The New Imperialism*, op. cit.

45 Arshad Abbasi, 'Military activity driving rapid glacier melting', Inter Press Service. Available online at: www.ipsnews.net/2009/12/ qa-military-activity-driving-rapid-glacier-mailing/; *Le Monde*, 12 June 2012.

46 See its website: www.idsa.in/taxonomy/term/124.

47 P. K. Gautam, 'Climate change and the military', *Journal of Defence Studies*, 3 (4), October 2009.

48 Duncan Freeman, 'The missing link. China, climate change, and national security', *Asia Paper*, Brussels Institute of Contemporary China Studies, 5 (8), 2010.

49 P. K. Gautam, 'An overview of ecological task forces (ETF) and ecological institutions of the Indian army', *Journal of the United Service Institution of India*, 139 (576), April–June 2009.

50 Benedict Anderson, *Imagined Communities: Reflections on the origin and spread of nationalism*, Verso, London, 1983.

51 Ramachandra Guha, 'Radical American environmentalism and wilderness preservation. A third world critique', loc. cit.

52 Ibid., p. 5.

53 Luis Martinez, *Violence de la rente pétrolière. Algérie-Irak-Libye*, Presses de Sciences Po, Paris, 2010, p. 37. On the redistribution of oil revenues in Nigeria and its implications for the form of the Nigerian state, see John Boye Ejobowah, 'Who owns the oil? Ethnicity in the Niger delta of Nigeria', *Africa Today*, 47 (1), 2000.

54 Ibid., p. 27.

55 Peter Coates et al., 'Defending nation, defending nature ? Militarized landscapes and military environmentalism in Britain, France, and the United States', loc. cit. See also Rachel Woodward, 'Khaki conservation. An examination of military environmentalist discourse in the British army', *Journal of Rural Studies*, 17, 2001.

56 For a look at the different ways in which military activity wreaks destruction on nature in times of both war and peace, see Gary E. Machlis and Thor Hanson, 'Warfare ecology', *BioScience*, 58 (8), September 2008.

57 Ibid., p. 72.

58 See John McNeill, 'Woods and warfare in world history', *Environmental History*, 9 (3), 2003, p. 400.

59 Welzer, *Climate Wars*, op. cit., p. 66.

60 Wayne Dwernychuk et al., 'Dioxin reservoirs in Southern Vietnam. A legacy of agent orange', *Chemosphere*, 47, 2007.

61 John McNeill, 'Woods and warfare in world history', loc. cit., p. 402.

62 Stephanie Pincetl, 'Some origins of French environmentalism. An exploration', loc. cit., p. 80.

63 Ibid., p. 394.

64 In this regard, see Paul Kennedy, *The Rise and Fall of Great Powers*, op. cit.

65 Bruce Podobnik, *Global Energy Shifts. Fostering Sustainability in a Turbulent Age*, Temple University Press, Philadelphia, 2006, p. 30.

66 Ibid., p. 84.

67 John McNeill, 'Woods and warfare in world history', loc. cit., p. 399.

68 Chris Pearson, 'Researching military landscapes. A literature review on war and the militarization of the environment', loc. cit., p. 116.

69 Jean-Paul Amat, 'Guerres et milieux naturels. Les forêts meurtries de l'est de la France, 70 ans après Verdun', *L'Espace géographique*, 3, 1987.

70 For a critique of the 'new wars' paradigm, see Edward Newman, 'The new wars debate. A historical perspective is needed', *Security Dialogue*, 35, 2004.

71 Martin van Creveld, *La Transformation de la guerre*, Éditions du Rocher, Paris, 2011, p. 110.

72 Thomas Hippler, 'Cent ans de bombardements aériens. Histoire d'une technique militaire et politique', *Revue des livres*, November 2011.

73 Mary Kaldor, *New and Old Wars. Organized Violence in a Global Era*, Polity Press, London, 2010. For an overall view of conflicts in recent decades, see Lotta Harbom and Peter Wallensteen, 'Armed conflict, 1989–2006', *Journal of Peace Research*, 44 (5), 2007.

74 Frédéric Gros, *États de violence. Essai sur la fin de la guerre*, Gallimard, Paris, 2006.

75 Mary Kaldor, *New and Old Wars*, op. cit., ch. 4.

76 Ibid., p. 97.

77 Nicos Poulantzas, *State, Power, Socialism*, op. cit., pp. 76–77.

78 See, in this regard, Jeremy Scahill, *Blackwater. The Rise of the World's Most Powerful Mercenary Army*, Serpent's Tail, New York, 2008.

79 *Le Monde*, 20 October 2012.

80 For a variant of this argument, see John Mearsheimer, *The Tragedy of Great Power Politics*, op. cit. See also Susan Watkins, 'The nuclear non-protestation treaty', *New Left Review*, 54, November–December 2008.

81 Thomas Schelling, 'An astonishing sixty years. The legacy of Hiroshima', *American Economic Review*, 96 (4), 2006, p. 929.

82 For a considered reflection on this theme, based on an analysis of the global uranium market, see Gabrielle Hecht, 'The power of nuclear things', *Technology and Culture*, 51, January 2010.

83 Philippe le Billon, 'The political ecology of war. Natural resources and armed conflicts', *Political Geography*, 20, 2001. See also Claude Serfati and Philippe le Billon 'Guerres pour les ressources : une face visible de la mondialisation', *Écologie & politique*, 34 (1), 2007.

84 Romain Lalanne, 'Quand la sécurité devient verte', *Revue de défense nationale*, 727, February 2010.

85 See Thomas Homer-Dixon, 'Environmental scarcities and violent conflict. Evidence from cases', *International Security*, 19 (1), 1994, p. 13. For a critique of the notion of 'resource wars', see David G. Victor, 'What resource wars?', *The National Interest*, November–December 2007.

86 Ibid., p. 14.

87 Thomas Homer-Dixon, 'Environmental scarcities and violent conflict. Evidence from cases', loc. cit., p. 32.

88 Thomas Homer-Dixon, quoted in Christian Parenti, *Tropic of Chaos*, op. cit. p. 63.

89 Karl Polanyi, *The Great Transformation*, Beacon Press, Boston, 1957.

90 Christian Parenti, *Tropic of Chaos*, op. cit., p. 65.

91 Luis Martinez, *Violence de la rente pétrolière*, op. cit., p. 14–15.

92 See Caitlin E. Werrel and Francesco Femia (eds.), *The Arab Spring and Climate Change*, Center for American Progress, New York, February 2013, p. 12. On this point, see also Gilbert Achcar, *The People Wants. A Radical Exploration of the Arab Uprising*, Saqi, London, 2013.

93 François Gemenne, *Géopolitique du changement climatique*, op. cit., ch. 3.

94 Harald Welzer, *Climate Wars*, op. cit.

95 François Gemenne, *Géopolitique du changement climatique*, op. cit., p. 83.

96 Romain Felli, 'Managing climate insecurity by ensuring continuous capital accumulation. "Climate refugees" and "climate migrants"', *New Political Economy*, 18 (3), 2013.

97 François Gemenne, *Géopolitique du changement climatique*, op. cit., p. 73.

98 Henrike Brecht et al., 'Sea-level rise and storm surges. High stakes for a small number of developing countries', loc. cit.

99 Christian Parenti, *Tropic of Chaos*, op. cit., p. 159.

100 *Rapport d'information sur l'impact du changement climatique en matière de sécurité et de défense*, presented by André Schneider and Philippe Tourtelier, op. cit., p. 46.

101 On this see Wendy Brown, *Walled States, Waning Sovereignty*, MIT Press, Boston, 2010.

102 Christian Parenti, *Tropic of Chaos*, op. cit., p. 184.

103 'National security and the threat of climate change', Center for Naval Analysis, loc. cit. p. 10.

104 Thomas Schelling, *The Strategy of Conflict*, Harvard University Press, Cambridge, 1980.

105 Will Steffen, Paul J. Cutzen and John McNeill, 'The anthropocene. Are humans now overwhelming the great forces of nature?', *Ambio*, 36 (8), 2007.

106 Raymond Boudon, *Effets pervers et ordre social*, PUF, Paris, 1977.

107 John Nagl and Christine Parthemore, 'A post-petroleum era', loc. cit.

108 'National security and the threat of climate change', Center for Naval Analysis, loc. cit., p. 26.

109 Gary E. Machlis and Thor Hanson, 'Warfare ecology', loc. cit., p. 729.

110 'National security and the threat of climate change', Center for Naval Analysis, loc. cit., p. 48.

111 On the connection between oil and organized crime, see, for example, Michael Watts (ed.), *Curse of the Black Gold. 50 Years of Oil in the Niger Delta*, Powerhouse, Brooklyn, 2008.

112 In this regard, see Bruce Podobnik, *Global Energy Shifts. Fostering Sustainability in a Turbulent Age*, op. cit. On this question, see also Timothy Mitchell, *Carbon democracy. Political Power in the Age of Oil*, Verso, London, 2011.

113 John Nagl and Christine Parthemore, 'A post-petroleum era', loc. cit.

114 See the Gallup survey at www.gallup.com/poll/1597/confidence-institutions.aspx.

115 Jean-François Mouhot, 'Past connections and present similarities in slave ownership and fossil fuel usage', *Climatic Change*, 105 (1–2), March 2011, p. 345.

116 For a good overview of this question, see Peter Schwartz, 'Abundant natural gas and oil are putting the kibosh on clean energy', *Wired*, 17 August 2012.

117 Richard F. Pittenger and Robert B. Gagosian, 'Global warming could have a chilling effect on the military', *Defense Horizons*, 33, October 2003.

118 Sharon Burke et al., 'Uncharted waters. The US Navy and navigating climate change', loc. cit., p. 21.

119 Ibid., p. 19.

120 Richard F. Pittenger and Robert B. Gagosian, 'Global warming could have a chilling effect on the military', loc. cit., p. 6.

121 National security and the threat of climate change', loc. cit., p. 37.

122 *Rapport d'information sur l'impact du changement climatique en matière de sécurité et de défense*, presented by André Schneider et Philippe Tourtelier, op. cit., p. 44.

123 Available online at www.independent.co.uk/voices/commentators/james-lovelock-the-earth-is-about-to-catch-a-morbid-fever-that-may-last-as-long-as-100000-years-5336856.html.

124 *Le Monde*, 9 March 2011.

125 On certain aspects of the intellectual history of the Cold War, such as it related to environmental questions, see Fabien Locher, 'Les pâturages de la guerre froide: Garrett Hardin et la "Tragédie des communs"', loc. cit.

126 Ronald E. Doel, 'Quelle place pour les sciences de l'environnement physique dans l'histoire environnementale?', loc. cit.

127 Ibid., p. 146.

128 Ibid., p. 144.

129 Charles K. Ebinger and Evie Zambetakis, 'The geopolitics of Arctic melt', *International Affairs*, 85 (6), 2009, p. 1216.

130 James Astill, 'The melting north', *The Economist*, 16 June 2012, p. 5.
131 Ibid.
132 Scott G. Borgerson, 'Arctic meltdown. The economic and security implications of global warming', *Foreign Affairs*, March–April 2008, p. 3–4.
133 Charles K. Ebinger and Evie Zambetakis, 'The geopolitics of Arctic melt', loc. cit., p. 1224.
134 Gwynne Dyer, *Climate Wars. The Fight for Survival as the World Overheats*, Oneworld publications, London, 2011.
135 James Astill, 'The melting north', op. cit., p. 10.
136 The *Canada First Defence Strategy,* which makes operational capacity in the Arctic one of the Canadian armed forces' six priorities, is available online at www.forces.gc.ca/en/about/canada-first-defence-strategy.page?#ql3.
137 Sharon Burke et al., 'Uncharted waters. The US Navy and navigating climate change', loc. cit. p. 35.
138 James Astill, 'The melting north', loc. cit., p. 12.
139 Charles K. Ebinger and Evie Zambetakis, 'The geopolitics of Arctic melt', loc. cit., p. 1219.
140 James Astill, 'The melting north', loc. cit., p. 11.
141 Karl Marx, *Grundrisse*, ch. 10, text available online at https://www.marxists.org/archive/marx/works/1857/grundrisse/ch10.htm.
142 See Elmar Altvater, 'The social and natural environment of fossil capitalism', *Socialist Register*, 43, 2007.
143 There is now a considerable literature on Marx's relation to ecology. Among various other possible perspectives, see John Bellamy Foster, *Marx's Ecology. Materialism and Nature*, Monthly Review Press, New York, 2000; Paul Burkett, *Marxism and Ecological Economics*, Brill, Leiden, 2006.
144 On Marxists' relation to Clausewitz, see Azar Gat, 'Clausewitz and the Marxists. Yet another look', *Journal of Contemporary History*, 27, 1992; Jacob Kipp, 'Lenin and Clausewitz. The militarization of Marxism, 1914–1921', *Military Affairs*, 49 (4), 1985; Bernard Semmel (ed.), *Marxism and the Science of War*, Oxford University Press, Oxford, 1981.
145 See Perry Anderson, *Considerations on Western Marxism*, NLB, London, 1976.

Conclusion: Game Over?

1 Walter Benjamin, *The Arcades Project*, Harvard University Press, Cambridge, MA, 2002, p. 917.

2 See Sasha Lilley et al., *Catastrophism. The Apocalyptic Politics of Collapse and Rebirth*, Merlin Press, London, 2012.
3 Serge Latouche, 'La décroissance est-elle la solution de la crise?', *Écologie & politique*, 40 (2), 2010; Jared Diamond, *Collapse. How Societies Choose to Fail or Succeed*, Viking, New York, 2005.
4 Antonio Gramsci, *Selections from the Prison Notebooks*, op. cit., p. 238.